East Lancashire Walks

Michael Smout

Published by Sigma Leisure – an imprint of
Sigma Press, 1 South Oak Lane, Wilmslow, Cheshire SK9 6AR, England.

British Library Cataloguing in Publication Data
A CIP record for this book is available from the British Library.

ISBN: 1-85058-595-4

Typesetting and Design by: Sigma Press, Wilmslow, Cheshire.

Cover photograph: Old Hall Farm, Bold

Maps: Alan Bradley

Photographs: the author

Printed by: MFP Design and Print

Preface

Encouraged by the response to my first book of West Lancashire Walks, I hope that these in East Lancashire are again useful in helping both organised groups and those who go out alone, or in twos or threes, to enjoy another of the less well known walking areas. These twenty walks fill in, without overlapping, the gap between my West Lancashire ones and those found in Mike Cresswell's book 'West Pennine Walks', another Sigma publication.

All the walks are circular and not more than six miles in length. In the comparatively short time since preparing my first book, certain details have changed, so, again in this one, I continue to give as many landmarks as possible along the way. The maps are marked CP for car park, S for stile, G for gate and FB for footbridge. The numbers on the map refer to the corresponding point in the written text.

The grid references are numbers which enable you to find a particular spot on the Ordnance Survey map. The first three numbers are Eastings referring to the numbers at the top and bottom of the map. The second three are Northings and are found at each side of the map. The most useful Ordnance Survey maps for walking are the Pathfinder $2\frac{1}{2}$" to 1 mile series.

My thanks are due again to Margaret Sadler for her secretarial help and to the staff at Sigma Press for it's help in enabling this book to see the light of day.

To those of you who enjoyed walking in West Lancashire, I think you will find the East just as rewarding. To those of you still out there somewhere, remember – if in doubt ask a policeman.

Michael Smout

Contents

Contents

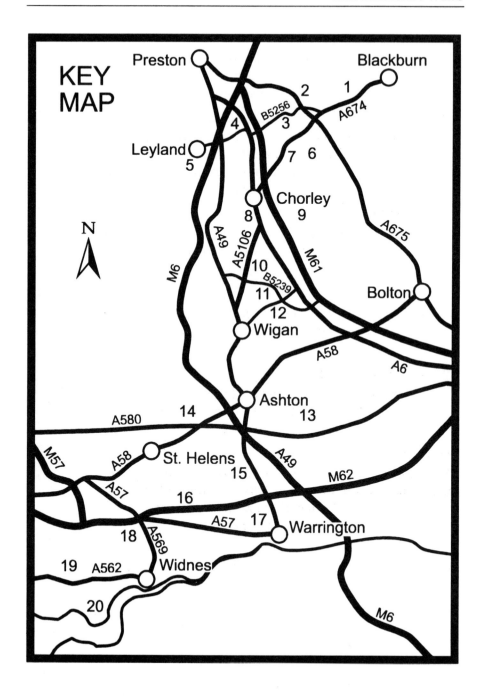

1. Witton Country Park

Witton Country Park is included in this field and forest walk very close to Blackburn.

Route: Witton – Billinge Hill – Yellow Hills – Butler's Delph – Witton.

Start: Main car park, Witton Country Park. Grid reference: 633 270.

Distance: 4½ or 3½ miles.

Duration: 2½ hours.

Map: SD 62/72

By car: Witton Country Park is situated on the west of Blackburn. The main entrance is from the A674 Preston Old Road, one mile out of the city. It is well signposted.

Refreshments: The Park Visitor Centre.

Witton Country Park covers 480 acres. It was the home of the Feilden family, whose estate was bought by Blackburn Corporation in 1946. Witton House was demolished in 1954. The Visitor Centre is housed in the old stables, harness room and coach house. The Centre also has a natural history room, changing exhibitions room, display of horse-drawn farm machinery, farm handtools and nineteenth-century horse drawn carriages. In addition there is a gift shop, cafeteria and toilet block. Opening times of the Centre are Monday – Saturday, 1.00pm – 5.00pm. Sundays, Bank holidays (except Christmas Day) 11.00am – 5.00pm. Closed Monday – Wednesday, October to March, except school holidays. The Park itself is open daily.

Other facilities are a children's corner and British small mammal centre, plus an athletics track.

1. From the car-park, walk round the left side of the athletics track to reach the building with the toilet block to its right. Go to the right along the metal road through an avenue of trees. The lily pond can be seen by turning to the left. As a track and

The old stables - only remains of Witton House

stream come in from the right, go through the posts, with another car park ahead.

Turn immediately left by the notice and follow the dirt track through the trees, with a stream on the left. As one path goes on to the right, go left over the footbridge and follow the path uphill through Big Cover Wood. Soon the path has wooden edges and there are steps at intervals along it. Pass over a footbridge and by a seat. The path splits for a short distance, but both tracks soon come back together. Fields can be seen through the trees to the left.

At a yellow-topped post do not turn right, but carry on until reaching a kissing gate. This leads into a field. A house can be seen ahead in the distance. Walk towards the waymarker ahead in the field. There are good views over to the left. Come to another kissing gate at the left corner of Higher Gardens Plantation.

Continue ahead. A second waymarker will be seen near the second of two trees in the field. At the stone wall, go up the

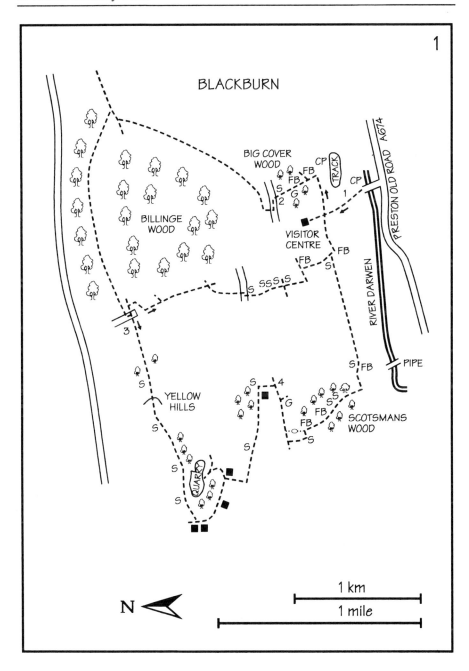

1

BLACKBURN

BIG COVER WOOD

CP
TRACK
FB
CP
S
G
2
1

BILLINGE WOOD

VISITOR CENTRE

FB
FB
S

S SSS S

3

RIVER DARWEN

PRESTON OLD ROAD   A674

S FB   PIPE

YELLOW HILLS

S   4
G
FB
FB
S
SCOTSMANS WOOD

S
S

QUARRY

S
S

N

1 km
1 mile

railed steps and then down those on the other side by the footpath sign. Up some more steps, you are on a narrow metal road by another footpath sign.

2. Turn left along the road and quickly right through a gap in the wall into Billinge Wood. A 'No horses' sign hangs in the trees. With one path going up to the left, take the one to the right which, at first, runs alongside the inside of the wall. The path ascends quite sharply. On reaching a white topped post with a fir tree symbol do not take the path to the left, but carry on, soon passing another similar post. At a cross road of paths, keep straight on by the red and yellow topped post. Pass a red topped post, somewhat hidden to the right.

On coming to a T-junction, turn right down a wide track and then next left by the red and blue topped post.

The path swings to the left. In the valley below are houses and a road. The path rises, passing a log seat on the left and then descends gradually. Just after a log seat on the right, go right at a split of paths. The path bears right and then left. After passing a big gully to the left, arrive at the end of a road.

3. Here the longer and shorter routes separate.

Longer route

On the opposite side of the road, where the fence joins the stone wall at the end of the metalled surface, go over an old stone stile. Immediately ahead is an old stone post. Cross the large field, aiming towards the lone tree that can be seen on the horizon. Cross a gully half way across the field and, with a pond to the left, come to the lone tree. To its right is a waymarked stile. Follow the waymark on the stile, straight ahead over the hillock. From the top, look down on the pond to the left. Continue on, over the sparse remains of a stone wall, towards a gate with a stile to the side of it. There is now a stile and a gate a little to the left of the corner of the field. From here, go towards the left-hand corner of the small fenced field, passing trees to the left. Over the stile go towards another in the left side of the next field. From this, descend through the tree the short distance to the lane below.

Emerge opposite to houses. Turn left along the lane, which swings to the left. Pass the farm to the right and continue until it soon reaches more farm outbuildings. It is possible to view the old quarry at Butler's Delph by taking the dirt track ahead up through the trees. As this becomes a grass track, turn sharp right up another path, passing the remains of a stone building. As the path splits, go upwards to the left to the edge of the quarry.

If not viewing the quarry, turn right through the farm buildings. As the track peters out, go to the opposite side of the field. You now pick up the old quarry track. Turn left to the stile in the corner of the field. Over it, passing a gate immediately on the right, the track start to descend. Keep as close to it as possible, since it can be overgrown in summer. At one point, it runs for a short section with a wall on either side. The track continues down through the trees. After passing along the back of a cottage, cross the small stile. Turn right down to the metal road.

4. Turn right again and, just past the left turn to Low Fold Farm go through the wicket gate by the large gate ahead. Follow the wide track across the centre of the field, reaching trees on the left. In the trees, a sign indicates 'Pleasington Playing Fields - ¾ mile'. Turn left along the right side of the stream, passing a pond. In the hedge ahead is a yellow marked stile. Over it, turn left and then right. Follow the path through open, sometimes overgrown ground, through two trees, until reaching a split of way.

Take the path to the left, passing immediately over a small footbridge. The path then passes over a low wall into woodland. Over a footbridge and stile, you will come in a few metres to another yellow marked stile.

The path goes to the left uphill, then down to a level. After this it drops sharply, as it swings to the right, passing two yellow topped posts. Over the small footbridge, turn left onto the field. Follow the edge of the field round to the left. Just beyond the left corner is a post (sometimes obscured). By it, go down the steps and over the footbridge and stile. Follow the path that goes ahead towards the left-hand corner of the opposite side of the large field. A few metres in from the left corner is a stile. From it, turn right over the stone bridge and left onto the field. Follow the left side of the field back towards the starting point.

Shorter Route

At the road, turn left for just a few metres and quickly left back into the wood. In another few metres turn right and soon right again. Ignore all paths coming in from the right or left. Pass a white post and a fir tree marker, after which the path drops quickly down, pass a log seat on the left. Continue along the path, until reaching a cross-roads, with a post on the right-hand corner. Turn right a short distance downhill. Pass under a bridge in the wall onto a metal road.

Do not go right over the cattle-grid, but turn left. A painted public footpath sign is high in the trees. Go down the steps and through the kissing gate. The path goes through an avenue of trees, with a stone wall on the right. After two stiles in quick succession, the path runs through a copse, now nearer to the fence on the left side. Two more stiles close to each other are reached, with a track running across the path to the farm to the right.

The route continues downhill, with a gully and pond to the right. At the T-junction turn left and then right down the steps and over the footbridge. With the stream in the deep gully to the right, follow the path downhill through Crow Wood to reach the field by the children's playing frame. Turn left along the edge of the field back to the car park.

2. Hoghton

The historic fortified hilltop mansion of Hoghton Tower and a beautiful stretch of the River Darwen with its gorge and weir, are highlights of this walk.

Route: Hoghton Village, Darwen Gorge – Hoghton Tower – Hoghton Village.

Start: Hoghton Village Hall. Grid reference 614 264.

Distance: 5½ miles.

Duration: 2½ hours

Map: SD 62/72.

Car: Hoghton Village Hall is on the A675 Blackburn to Preston Road, about 100 metres on the Blackburn side of the Black Bull pub.

Refreshments: The Black Bull, Hoghton and the Boatyard Inn, Riley.

---

1. From the village hall, turn right along the road. There are cottages on the left. Opposite is Lane Side Farm. Attached to the farm is a now derelict cottage. Immediately beyond the cottage and opposite the copse on the other side of the road, a footpath sign points down a wide track. This track, with at first a wire fence to the left and the side of the derelict cottage on the right, then bends right through the farm buildings. As you reach the recreation ground and tennis courts, the track bends left to a gate, with a stile to its right.

The track now has a fence or hedge on both sides, leading in a short time to another gate and stile. Passing various gateways on the right, keep to the left of the hedge of tall trees. After these the path drops into a small valley and then up the other side. Keep the fence to the right as the path descends again towards the gate at the corner of the field. Over to the right a farm can be seen in the distance.

At the gate, there is a pond in the field to the right. Do not go through the gate and over the footbridge, but over the stile to the left. Follow the tall hedge on the right up to another stile. This leads into a very large field, with the outbuildings of Hatchwood Farm higher up to the left. Still keeping the hedge to the right, you will come to a copse. A footbridge goes over the stream into the woodland, but keep instead ahead along the left edge of the copse, which has concrete posts along its boundary.

Beyond the copse, come to the corner of the field and go over the stile onto the narrow metal lane. To the left, the lane goes to Hatchwood Farm, but keep ahead through the usually open gate, which has a stile by it. Another farm can be seen over to the right.

2. At the end of the lane, turn left along the road. Millstone Farm is immediately to the left. Look for the footpath sign which points to the left of the farm barn. Go through the gap by the gate, through the two old gateposts ahead and up the wide grass track to a stile and plank ahead. In the field, keep to the left of the trees and gully. Pass across a track, an old bridge and derelict stone building. Immediately ahead is a stile in the hedge, by an old gate and footpath sign.

Turn left up the narrow sunken road. Opposite the farm on the brow of the hill, turn right through the gap by the gate. Keep to the right of the hedge and poles going downhill. To the right in the field are two small sheds and an old windmill. As the buildings ahead come near, go over a stile to the left in the hedge. Turn right, with the hedge now on the right. It is a short distance to the stone stile and bridge onto the road just beyond Silcock Farm. Do not go over the stile opposite, but turn left along the road. Pass by Scale Hill Farm on the left, then a bungalow on the right. Soon after the horses warning sign, you meet Dover Lane coming in from the left, opposite a farm. Turn right towards Brindle.

Continue along the road until reaching a sharp right bend On the left, in the hedge, is a footpath sign and stile. Over the stile, continue ahead, with the hedge and fence to the right. Cross a footbridge, which can sometimes be hidden from sight

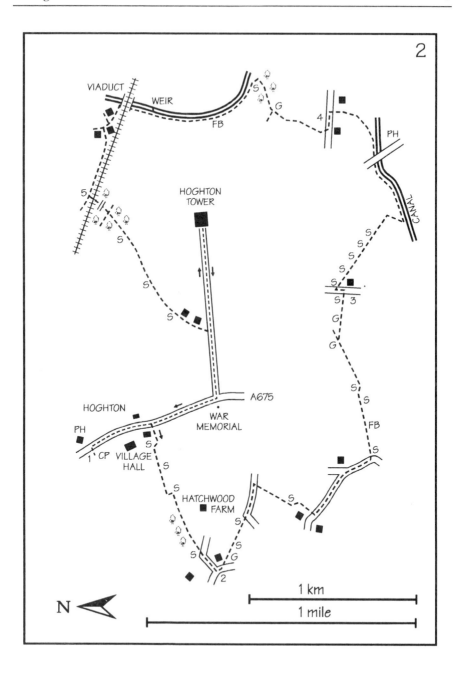

in summer until reaching it. Keep ahead, until arriving at a stile by a gate.

In the next field, go forward a short distance to stile in a fence. Then continue ahead with the fence to the left. Eventually, the fence gives way to trees on the left. A few metres further on is a black gate. From here, aim for the gate about half way between the hedge on the left and the ridge to the right. From the gate, go across the field half right towards a gate and stile to the right of the houses. This brings you onto a road.

3. Cross the road to the pavement on the far side and walk to the left. After passing the house called Westleigh, turn right at the footpath sign over the stile by the gate. A short grass track arrives quickly at another gate and stile. Over in the field, stay to the left of the fence, passing a brick building en route. At the end of the field, there is a stile a few metres in from the corner. From here, with the fence still on the right, the path continues an up and down course. After crossing four stiles in wire fences, it drops down to a stream. The M65 can be seen quite near on the right. At the stream, cross the double stile and bridge. Then follow the wooden fence to the right, until it reaches a stile, on the other side of which is the canal towpath.

With a high hedge to the left and high ground on the other side of the canal, walk to the left until reaching the road bridge. If you want a break at the Boathouse Inn on the other side of the canal, take the path immediately beyond the bridge that doubles back to the road. Otherwise, keep on the towpath for a few more metres. Just by the visitors' mooring sign, follow the footpath sign to the left. This path can sometimes be somewhat overgrown in summer and therefore not best for a rainy day. (The alternative is to follow the main road (A625) from the bridge into Riley green and then turn right onto the A6061 until reaching the house before the transmitters. This is about half a mile). The path gradually goes away from the canal, with a hedge to the right. Then there is a stone wall on the right, after which there is a hedge on both sides. After a

derelict cottage on the right, the path comes onto the A6061.
Turn left, passing the transmitters, to a detached house.

4. Opposite to it, there is a footpath sign. Walk along the wide
lane, which has a high hedge to the right. At a sharp left-hand
bend, the lane leads on towards a house. On the right of the
bend is a gate, besides which is a wicket gate. Go through this
and follow the farm track as it goes to the left, through the
field, towards the woodland.

From a gate with a stile, the track descends through a short
stretch of fenced woodland. At the field going down to the
river, bear left down to a ladder stile on the river bank. From
the stile, the path no runs along the left bank of the river. It
passes over a footbridge, before coming to the weir. From here,
it continues along the edge of the gorge. You go over a stone
bridge and then an iron bridge. After a wall on the left-hand
side, the lofty railway viaduct is reached.

The path now bears left, away from the river, with a garden
fence to the right. At the road coming in from the right by the

Weir in River Darwen Gorge

cottages, keep ahead. After a hundred metres, leave the road, to follow a signed bridlepath that ascends between the houses. After a while, there is a wall on either side. Pass a derelict cottage on the right, arriving at a stile by a gate. The wide track now runs parallel to the railway fence. The fence to the right comes to an end.

5. With the road bridge ahead in the distance, turn left, across the railway, through the white gate, by the 'Stop, Look and Listen' sign. From another white gate on the opposite side, a path goes up through the woodland, passing under an old bridge. At a cross track, there is a footpath sign, which points up through the woods, bearing right. (Not the track at right angles). The path reaches a stile by a high stone wall. Passing through a field, keep to the edge of the wall.

Soon after a door in the wall marked 'Private', a stile leads into the next field. Keep by the wall, which is now lower, passing a wired up gateway. After a longish stretch, pass a solitary tree besides the remains of an old stile. Not long after this, there is a stile by a gate. This takes you ahead along a metal lane by some stone cottages to come onto the main access route to Hoghton Tower.

The tower can be seen to the left at the top of the hill. It is the seat of Sir Bernard de Hoghton and has been the ancestral home of the Hoghton family since William the Conqueror. It has a great Banqueting Hall where the 'Loin of Beef' was knighted by King James I in 1617 and where William Shakespeare started his working life. It also has a Tudor Well house and underground passages and dungeons. The Tower is open from Easter to the end of October on Sundays 1.00pm – 5.00pm and in July and August Tuesday to Thursday 11.00am – 4.00pm in addition.

If you are not visiting the Tower, then turn right down the tree-lined road, with its wide grass verge and low wooden posts at the side of the road. Emerge with care onto the main road, opposite to the war memorial. After only a short distance to the right, you return to the village hall on the left of the road.

3. Brindle

An attractive walk through Withnell Fold, with good views of the West Pennine Moors.

Route: Route – Top o' th' Lane – Withnell Fold – Brindle.

Start: Village Hall Car Park, Brindle. Grid reference: 599 242.

Distance: 4 miles.

Duration: 2 hours.

Maps: SD 42/52 and SD 62/72

By car: Brindle is situated on the B5256 1./12 miles north-east of the M61. Turn right by the church. The village hall is a few hundred metres down the road, on the left opposite the phone box.

Refreshments: Cavendish Arms opposite the church.

---

1. Turn left from the car-park along the road, passing Prospect Cottage on the left. Immediately beyond St James Primary School on the right, a sign points you through a gate and along a short track. The school playing field is on the left. Go over the stile and walk left at an angle of 45° towards the left end of a row of small trees in a gully. Here find a stile in the corner of a field.

Then follow the left edge of the field. There is a steady ascent, first of all by a line of trees in a gully, followed by a barbed wire fence. There are now good views over to the left towards Darwen Tower and Winter Hill. Reach another stile and continue uphill with the fence still on the left. A gate and water trough is passed before reaching a stile, with a couple of large stones by it.

Aim ahead to the left of the clump of trees which surround a pond. A stile will be seen in the wire fence. Pass the small gully and make for the fence and line of bushes along the right edge of the field.

At the next stile in the corner of the field, you will come onto the road at Top o' th' Lane. Go to the right, with a red telephone kiosk and the renovated Top o' th' Lane farm on the left. At the end of the line of cottages and houses on the right, a sign for a bridleway and a footpath will be seen on the left.

2. (A short diversion is possible here for a viewpoint. Turn right up the concrete road, with a high stone wall on the right. As the lane goes sharply right, go ahead, through the wooden gate, along the track which goes up between stone walls. After the short ascent, there is a wide opening in the wall. There are good views across the lowland plain. From here return to the original point).

From the road turn left along the signposted lane. This is a wide hedged farm track, which steadily descends. Pass an old water supply culvert on the right. Soon after the track turns into a concrete one, it bends sharply to the right. This is the place to be watchful, because the stile is in the hedge in the corner of the field straight ahead as the bends start. It can be obscured by summer vegetation.

Keep to the left edge of the field, which has a fence interspersed with hedge and trees along it. Across to the right will be seen Walmsley Fold Farm. Soon after passing a stile on the left, turn right at the far end of the field, passing the gate into the next field and following the fence to the stile. Then follow the well worn track downhill through the middle of a large field. Soon, a gate will be seen ahead, with a stile at the side. From the stile, it is only a short distance, walking slightly to the right, to the footbridge over the narrow River Lostock.

Pause at the bridge and a canal bridge will be seen up the hill slightly to the right up the slope in front of you. The next stile, which gives access to the Leeds-Liverpool canal, is hidden in the trees, just to the left of the bridge. Rather than a direct assault up the steepish slope, go straight ahead. As you ascend, you will find a track that goes up through the bushes to the stile and onto the canal towpath.

3. From Simpson Fold Bridge, go left along the towpath. There

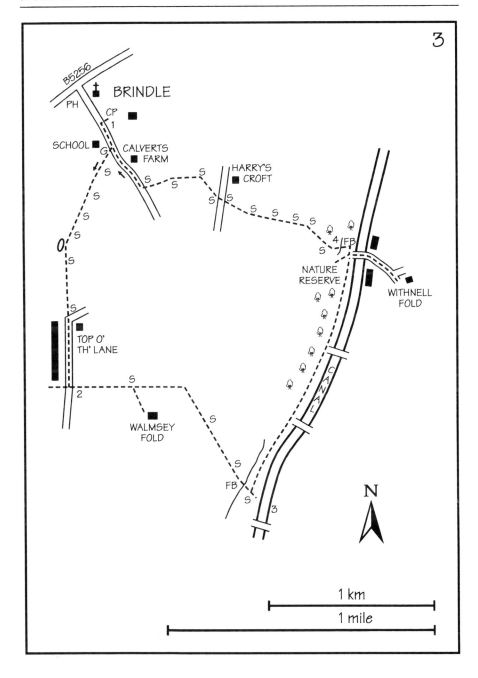

Cavendish Arms and church, Brindle

is a steep wooded hillside on the far side of the canal and good
views across to the left. Pass under two bridges. Now on the
left is Ramsbottom Wood. After a stone wall to your left, come
to a third bridge. New houses and also the old mill will be
seen on the far bank. Having gone under the bridge, immediately turn left onto the wide canal side track.

If you have the time, go over the bridge and up the cobbled
road that bears right into Withnell Fold village. Immediately
in front of you, you will see the old Reading Room, now a
private house. Turn left and in a short distance you will come
to the village stocks.

Returning over the bridge, on the left is the gate into the nature
reserve. If you wish to add about a mile to the walk, it is
possible to follow a trail through the woodland.

4. To continue the walk, follow the footpath sign that takes you
from the canal side down the narrow cobbled fenced path
down through the trees. Go past the pond and over the little
bridge across the juvenile River Lostock. The cobbled path

continues upwards to a stile in the fence. Then follow the left-hand side of the field as it goes upwards. You will see a pond over on the right and Lower Hiltons Farm in the distance. Cross another stile and walk the short distance, by the fence, across another field. Do not take the waymarked stile on the left, but continue to a stile directly ahead.

Follow the fence as it swings to the right until, eventually, there is a stream and trees to your left. Soon after passing a little valley which goes off to the right, arrive at the stile into the next field. Still stay on the left side of the field. To the right is Harry's Crofts Farm. At the stile and sign cross the narrow road to the stile and sign almost immediately opposite. Keep the hedge to the left. Do not aim for the gate you will soon see ahead, but keep to the hedge as it bears left towards a stile in the left corner of the field.

There is a short downhill descent, keeping to the hedge, down to a stile that still has the remnants of the old stone construction. Go directly uphill. For a few metres there are trees to the left, but then go straight across the field. The next stile and sign will be seen a few metres from the left-hand corner of the opposite hedge.

Turn right along the road. Pass Calverts Farm and the school warning sign to arrive back at the car park.

4. Cuerden Country Park

A Walk round the country park, the valley of the River Lostock.

Route: Clayton Bridge – Cuerden Hall – Cam Lane – Lower Wood End –
               Clayton Bridge.

Start: Country Park car park, Clayton Bridge. Grid reference: 567 228

Distance: 4 miles.

Duration: 2 hours.

Maps: SD 42/52.

By car: Cuerden Country Park main car park is situated on the B5256
               between Clayton-le-Woods and Clayton Green.

Refreshments: Ley Inn.

1. From the car park, take the central path. This is a well worn
one. At first it goes through the middle of the field and then
reaches the right bank of the river. Over to the left of the river
can be seen woods and to the right of them, a high bank. Pass
by a stone ford. As the trees get nearer on the right, there are
willows along the river bank.

At the split of paths take the one to the left, which goes over
a footbridge. Turn left along the wide path. Do not turn first
right, but continue to the river bank, where there is another
stone ford. Do not cross, but follow the dirt path along the
right bank of the river. Do not take the path that goes to the
right, but continue along the bank edge, through the trees.
Eventually the path swings to the right away from the river.
After a short distance, you come to open land. Go straight
across to the woods opposite. A dirt path comes from the right
and, at the entrance to the woods, one goes to the left towards
a seat. But pick up the gravel track from the right as it enters
the wood. In a few metres turn left at a signpost and follow
the wide track through the trees.

After a post with a red arrow on it, the track comes into the

Stepping stones at River Lostock

open, with the river and a seat on the left. After passing under telegraph wires, you come to a park information board. Just ahead is a ford and a bridge across the river.

2. The picnic tables make it a good place for a stop. If you wish to get a good view of Cuerden Hall, cross the bridge and follow the path going up to the right. Soon after it swings left, the Hall can be seen across the fields to the left. Return back over the bridge, to the information board. From the information board, turn right towards the trees. Ignore a path to the left, just before the main track slopes upwards. At the top of the short slope, turn left up the steps with green railings. Turn right along the side of the lake and then left along a second side. Just opposite an island in the lake, follow the path as it bends to the right.

Cross the footbridge and go to the steps ahead in the field. At the top of these, turn left at the junction of paths. Follow the field up by the fence to the gate. At the triangle of paths turn right. After a short uphill section, pass a seat and later a pond on the right. Then comes the long fence surrounding Cam Lane Cottage. At the front entrance of the cottage, it can be seen that the word 'cottage' is a euphemism.

You now continue ahead on the wider Cam Lane, which passes through Green Wood. The lane crosses a path coming up steps from the left. After ponds on the right and the backs of houses on the left, pass a bungalow and farm entrance on the right, to arrive at the road at the entrance to Dovecote.

3. Cross the road opposite the old cottage and turn right. Just after Glenmore, the pavement fortunately rises high above the busy road. After walking downhill for a few minutes and as the fence comes to an end, turn left up the wooden steps.

Continue upwards through the open ground to a gate. This brings you to a narrow road with a housing estate to the left. Turn right for a few metres towards some bungalows. Just before reaching them, turn left through a gate and right along the path. This, passing a clearing and seat to the right, comes

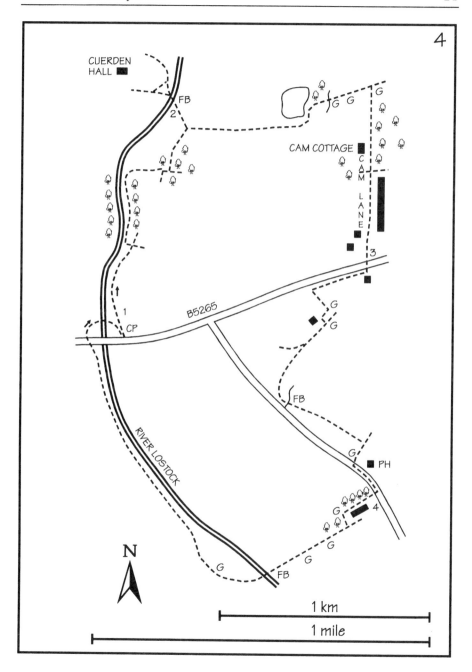

into open ground. At the split of paths, take the one going to the left downhill rather than the one ascending to the right. Pass steps to the right and go down a couple as the path bends sharply to the left. Through the trees, come to a footbridge, just beyond a gate which leads right onto the road. Over the bridge, the path ascends, passing a seat to the left. At the T-junction, with a seat opposite, turn right. Go through a space with seats, pass a table on the right and, through the gate, arrive at the road. Turn left towards the Ley Inn.

Just beyond the inn, turn right at a footpath sign, immediately after a metal farm road. The path travels along the high back fences of a housing estate. There are trees on the right, through which the farm can be glimpsed. Going through a gate, cross the open space to a T-junction. Turn right down the wide path. After passing through the trees, there is a fence on the right. Go through a gate and across an open field to another gate, which in turn leads, after crossing wooden planks, to a foot-bridge over the river. Ignore two tracks coming in from the left, as the path bends to the right over a flat wooden bridge. Arrive at a gate by a seat plus a quarry sign. The path now continues with a fence to the left and the valley through the trees to the right. Signs for the Clayton Hall Sand Company will be seen along the path to the left. After a gate and hedge on the right, go under the wires to another gate. Now with bushes on either side of the path, go through a gate and onto Town Brow Road.

Go through the gate on the opposite side of the road. Follow the path to the right towards the river. Cross the stepping stone and continue the short distance back to the car park. If the river is running high, instead go right along the road to the car park on the left.

5. Leyland

A Walk south of Leyland, including Worden Hall, the home of the Council for the Protection of Rural England.

Route: Worden Hall – Euxton Hall, Runshaw Moor – Worden Hall.

Start: Visitor Centre, Worden Hall, Leyland. Grid reference 536 208.

Distance: 5 miles.

Duration: 2½ hours.

Maps: SD 41/51 and 42/52

By car: Access to the Worden Hall car park from the road at grid reference 544 207.

Refreshments: Worden Hall Café and Bay Horse, Euxton.

1. From the Visitor Centre, turn right in the direction of the maze sign, then immediately left to go back through the gardens parallel to the Visitor Centre, passing the palm house on your left. At the end of the gardens, turn left and then right through the open gate. The formal gardens are on the right. As the metal road goes away to the left and with another path to the right, take the wide path ahead. The path goes downhill, with another one crossing it at an angle.

At the bottom of the slope, cross the footbridge over the River Yarrow. Turn left and, going by the stone arch over the river, cross the footbridge over the weir. Do not take the path ahead, but the one going to the right. This takes you over a plank across a narrow stream and along a winding path through the trees.

After crossing a small dry gully and a dead tree across the way, join a wider path coming in from the left. Go on along the edge of the wood, bearing right and then left again. A few metres after the corner of the field, do not take the path continuing along the edge of the field, but go left over the deep gully and up into the next field.

Palm House

Still continue with the stream and woods to the left. Ignore the footbridge to the left and go on until the road bridge is reached. Just beyond the corner of the field, go up onto the road at the end of the bridge wall. Walk right along the pavement on the other wide until you see a footpath sign on the left. There a log across the entrance to the path to prevent vehicular traffic. The path goes for about a hundred metres through a wide area, with a copse on the left. It reaches the access road to Holt Farm by a fir hedge.

With the gate leading to the farm, plus a security warning to the left, cross to the stile immediately opposite. Go across the small paddock to the stile in the right corner by some trees. Do not take the wide track that goes to the right. Walk along the right edge of the field, passing a pond en route. At the end of the field, turn left along a wide farm track coming in from the right. One the right are playing fields, complete with goal posts.

At the corner of the field, pass a junction box and old stile, as

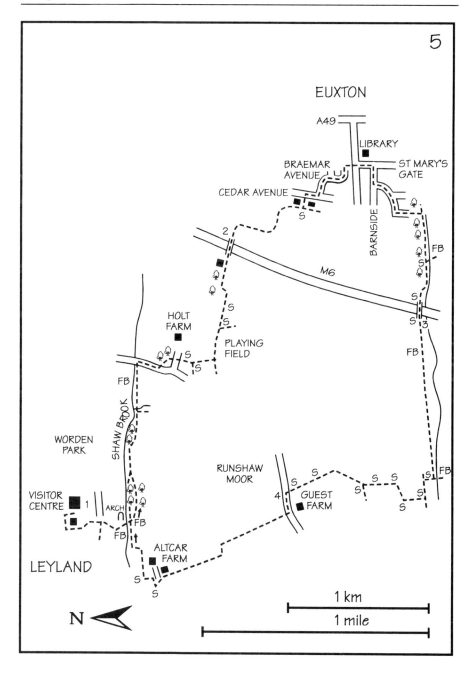

5

EUXTON

A49

LIBRARY

BRAEMAR
AVENUE

ST MARY'S
GATE

CEDAR AVENUE

S

BARNSIDE

FB

2

S

M6

S

FB

HOLT
FARM

S

S

S

PLAYING
FIELD

S

S

FB

3

S

FB

S

FB

SHAW BROOK

WORDEN
PARK

RUNSHAW
MOOR

S

S

S

S

FB

VISITOR
CENTRE

1

ARCH

FB

4

GUEST
FARM

S

S

FB

LEYLAND

ALTCAR
FARM

S

S

N

1 km

1 mile

the track now continues between hedges. As the track bends sharply right, there is a stile to the left. The path now runs between the hedge and a wire fence. Go over another stile into the next field. Keep to the left of this field. The path bends to the left and then to the right by a fenced off copse. After some farm buildings on the left, pass over the motorway bridge. There is a 32 tons weight limit, which hopefully excludes most walkers.

A local farmer passed on the interesting information that when the bridge was first built, some expensive motorway equipment was lost because of the quicksand thereabouts. It is still there buried beneath the sand.

2. Beyond the bridge continue along the farm track, passing the 'no footpath' sign on a gate in the fence on the right. The track bears to the right, now with no fence on the right. After going under telegraph wires, it then swings to the left. Just before this bend to the right is a pile of concrete. This was the war time site of a gun emplacement, because of the all round view. The old shelters under the ground have long been filled in.

The track goes through an old gateway and then goes to the right across open ground towards the houses. Soon after it runs parallel with the houses, turn left over a stile that leads down a short alleyway to the road. At the road end there is a sign pointing back to Holt Brow.

There is now an unavoidable street route through Euxton for a few minutes. From the signpost, turn right along Cedar Avenue. After passing Yew Tree Avenue to the right go second left along Briar Avenue. This bends to the right. At the cul-de-sac, turn left and then right down the alleyway which runs a few metres to Runshaw Road. (If refreshments are needed at this point, simply turn left to the Bay Horse by the traffic lights). Cross the road and go down St Mary's Gate, which has the library on the left-hand corner. Turn right along Barnside and left into Greenside (no name plate). Pass a green on the left and then turn left down the second road on the left, which is a cul-de-sac.

The path is hidden in the left-hand corner at the end of the short road. Go down the steps to the stream. Turn right and walk through the trees along its right edge. Ignore all paths coming down the slope from the right. Immediately after passing the footbridge, continue ahead over a stile into a field. The path stays to the right of the stream, which meanders through the meadow. Do not take the stone bridge that crosses the stream.

The far bank rises and there is a fence high up on it. Soon after going through a clump of trees, at the fork of paths, take the one that goes to the right up the slope. At the top of the slope, with new houses visible behind, aim for the motorway bridge ahead. There are stiles on either side of this yellow construction.

3. After the stile on the far side of the bridge, cross the middle of the field straight ahead to the low stone bridge. From this, go gradually leftwards across the field to the stream and then follow it along the edge of the bank. The right side of the field has a line of trees along it. At the way marked stile at the end of the fields, go right, not left over the footbridge. At the corner of the field, turn left and again follow the edge of the field until you see the hedge of another field coming in from the right.

Go up the short pull to the stile on the right. Go the couple of metres back right to the edge of the field. Turn left at the corner and follow the gully and trees a good distance, until the corner of the field is reached where it comes to a point. Over the stile, keep to the hedge and, after a few metres, go left over a high stile. Then walk across the centre of the large meadow. By aiming towards the barns in the distance, you will soon see a low stile in the hedge ahead, by a lone tree.

Cross the stile and footbridge and go straight across the smaller field towards another stile and footbridge. Then follow the hedge to the corner of the field. Turn left and then left again at the next corner. To the left in the field are what for most of the year are dry ponds.

At the end of this third section of hedge, having walked a good way round the perimeter of the field, arrive at a stile and footbridge. Cross the next field to the stile immediately opposite and arrive at the road by the footpath sign.

4. Walk left along the wide verge. Opposite to the entrance to Guest Farm, take the narrow metal road, with the large house to the left of it. After passing a copse on the left and with Runshaw Hall to be seen over the fields to the right, the road continues with just one small zig-zag. Having passed through an open gate and the back of a building, the road turns right into Altcar Farm.

Straight ahead, just as the bend begins, is a stile by a gate. Over it turn right along the edge of the railed field towards the farm. Then bear left along the back of the building for a few metres and right along a tall tin fence. At the end of it is another stile. Go right over it into a field. Aim for the far left corner as it slopes to the left. Just before the left corner is a stile. This lead some metres through small trees onto a path by the river. Turn right along the edge of the stream until reaching the footbridge. Over the footbridge bear left up the wide track back to Worden Hall.

6. Brinscall

A riverside walk, an isolated cricket field and the fringe of Anglezarke combine to make this a delightful walk.

Route: Brinscall – White Coppice – Anglezarke – Brinscall.

Start: Brinscall Baths car park. Grid reference. 628 214.

Distance: 4 miles.

Duration: 2 hours.

Maps: SD 61/71 and SD 62.72.

By car: Brinscall is on the A674, four miles east of Chorley. At the foot of the hill in the village, turn into Lodge Lane from School Lane. The baths and car park are immediately to the left.

Refreshments: The Oak Tree and the Cricketers public houses plus the Fish and Chip shop in School Lane adjacent to Lodge Lane.

---

1. From the car park, turn left along the road, with the reservoir to the left and houses, giving way to bungalows, on the right. After passing the pumping station on the left and the last bungalow on the right, the road becomes a track through the woodland. At the crossroad of tracks, where the one to the right goes under the disused railway, go straight ahead over the cattle grid. The track is metal for a little way, but as it enters woodland again, becomes cobbled. There is a wall in the trees on the right.

As the track goes on through the gateway into the private grounds of Drakeshead, the old lodge, turn right over the waymarked stile by the tree with the 'public footpath' notice on it. The path bears to the left through the trees, with a fence and then a wall on the left.

Go over the stile, which is at the end of the garden of a stone house. Follow the path across the middle of the field. The next stile is at a stream just to the left of a very small fir plantation. A path goes off to the right towards a waymarked stile. Do take this, but go straight ahead, along the side of the fence, passing under the boughs of a tree en route. Over the stile, turn right along the path which runs alongside the fence of a copse. There is a wire fence on the right of the path. At the end of the path, turn left to reach a bridge over the stream, known as the Goit.

2. Turn right and walk along the path on the nearside of the stream. Over on the far side, the heights of Anglezarke begin to rise. The path stays by the stream and winds its way through glades of trees.

At the next bridge, the path swings away to the right, through trees and bushes. To the left, you can get a first glimpse, across the reservoir of White Coppice and its cricket field. After crossing a stream and a stile, walk along between the edge of the reservoir and the little hill, called The Lowe. At the end of the reservoir, turn left across the stream, over the low stile and down the pathway between the railings on the left and the fence of the beautiful garden on the right.

Cricket ground at White Coppice

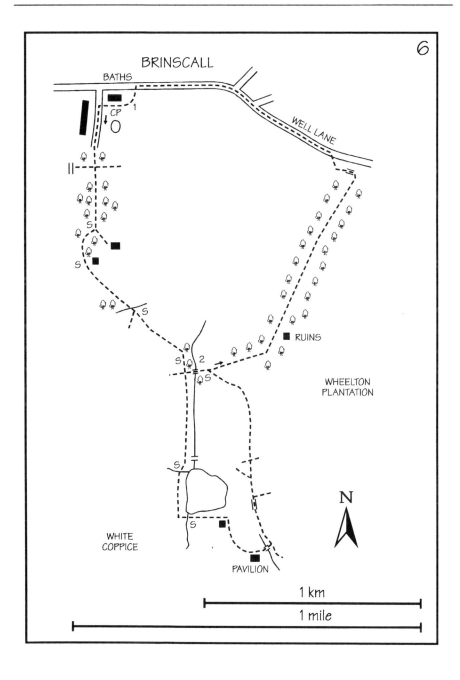

BRINSCALL

BATHS

CP 1

WELL LANE

S

S

S

S 2 S

RUINS

WHEELTON PLANTATION

S

S

WHITE COPPICE

S

PAVILION

N

1 km

1 mile

3. You are now at the cricket field at White Coppice. Turn right along the track in front of the two cottages and follow the white rails of the field around to the pavilion. This is a delightful spot, in the shadow of the hills, to stop and relax for a while. It is peaceful and quiet, except at weekends when matches are in progress. On match days, the pavilion toilets are available for use and there are refreshments on sale. The return section of the walk is near to the opposite bank of the Goit, but with much more of a hill walk feel to it.

From the cricket pavilion, cross the bridge over the stream. Turn left and follow the stone path, which goes up towards the bridge with a stone seat built into it. From here is a good view back to White Coppice. Do not take the path to the right, with the sign for Belmont Road and Brinscall, but continue ahead, parallel to the reservoir and then the stream, although high above them.

There is a stone wall to the left. Cross the remains of a wall ahead. As the paths divide, do not take the one descending to the left, but the one which continues ahead to cross a sunken track with walls built into it. From here the path goes gradually upwards, still further away from the stream.

Reaching a tree, cross another broken wall. The well-worn path goes on, with a ruined wall as its left boundary, with occasional trees along the way. Between it and the steam, way below, is an area of marshland.

The path gradually begins to descend, until the trees become more numerous. As the path almost reaches the level of the surrounding land, there is a split in the paths. It does not make any difference which one you take, since both arrive, in a short distance, at the same destination. There is a stile, just to the right of the bridge over the stream and on the edge of the wood plantation.

The remainder of the route from here involves a steady, uphill climb. There is an escape route at this point. By crossing the bridge, you are at point 2 on the outward part of the walk. Simply follow the outward way back into Brinscall.

Otherwise, from the stile at the bridge, turn right on the wide track that goes through Wheelton Plantation. The dreary look of the fir trees at first is compensated for later on by a mixture with native species of trees. The track becomes narrower as it reaches a stone wall, where it turns to the left. Soon it passes the ruins of an old house, named Heather Lea. Continuing along the track, it passes another ruin on the left. Do not take any paths down through the woods. After a stone wall along the left of the track, go left over a bridge, above a gorge, and through the gate, onto Well Lane.

The lane descends fairly steeply, until, after passing a cottage to the right, you turn left and, shortly after that, left again into School Lane. Just before the Fish and Chip shop, turn left into the car park.

7. Wheelton

A walk, including a steady uphill section, includes a beautiful series of four locks.

Route: Wheelton – Top Lock – Denham Hall – Wheelton.

Start: The War Memorial, Wheelton Village Centre. Grid reference: 211 601

Distance: 4½ miles.

Duration: 2¼ hours.

Maps: SD 42-52 and SD 62/72

Car: Wheelton village centre is ¼ mile west of the A674 Chorley to Blackburn Road. Two miles north east of Chorley.

Refreshments: Red Lion, Wheelton and The Top Lock Inn at the locks.

---

1. From the war memorial, turn right into Kenyons Lane. Walk on the pavement on the left of the road, passing a row of houses. On the other side is a field. Looking back you can see a farm, perched high up on the hill behind the village.

The tall chimney of Denton Mill rises in the distance ahead of you. As the pavement comes to an end, the road turns sharply left, opposite to the Wheelton boat yard. Passing a small brick building on the left, the road runs parallel to the canal, soon reaching Top Lock Inn at the T Junction. Turn right along Copthurst Road, over the canal bridge. Go left, down the steps onto the tow path, walking away from Top Lock.

After a house to the left, the towpath goes through open country-side. Pass two locks, with the accompanying short stretch of stone path, which brings you onto a lower level. At the next bridge, go up the steps, across Town Lane. Take the steps opposite, with a small stone building to the right, back onto the towpath. Then there is a series of four locks close together. Soon you come to two bridges. Do not take the

Locks at Wheelton

left-hand one across the canal to where there is a signpost, pointing to Blackburn and Leeds on the left and Wigan and Liverpool to the right.

Go over the bridge to the right which goes over the river as it joints the canal.

2. There is a choice of ways here:

Either:

From the towpath go back under the bridge on the stone path. This goes along the left bank of the river. There is a hedge to the left and, at one point, a short row of trees to the right. There are two footpath signs incongruously planted in the river. Eventually, the path, still by the river, comes to a large open space in front of houses and a road.

Or:

Continue ahead along the towpath passing the cottage on the right. There is housing on the other bank of the canal. At the next bridge, go up the slope onto the road. Immediately turn right through the gate by the footpath sign. The wide track runs parallel to the canal path you have just come along, across the open space to the right. There is a fence and trees to the left. Look for a stile on the left, with a little wooden indicator pointing to it. This has obviously been placed there by the owner of the cottage to which the track proceeds.

Keeping to the right of the fence, climb gradually upwards. Pass a gate space on the left, and come to another stile in the corner of the field. A waymarker points at an angle across the field. Follow its direction. The next stile is difficult to see, until you get nearer to it.

Over it, keep to the left of the hedge to reach a pond. Follow it round to the right. It will be possible to see the motorway footbridge ahead. On reaching it, do not cross, but follow the fence and then trees upwards away from the motorway. When the corner of the field is reached, the stile will be seen, hidden down a small slope. Continue downhill, still keeping to the right of the hedge. At the bottom of the hill, go through the gate and along the short, wide track to the large open space.

3. Here the shorter and long route join. Go left onto the road, by the footpath sign. Turn right along the road. As it bends sharply to the right and the pavement comes to an end, turn left, at the footpath sign, along the metal road. After passing a row of stone cottages on the left, the lane goes through countryside. Houses can be seen ahead. Care now needs to be taken, because there is a stile on the left, half hidden behind a small bush. Go over it into the field and then a few metres up, take the stile to the right. Follow the path as it wends its way through a higher gorse ridge, under the telegraph wires. As the ridge continues, there are good views over to the right.

Next take a stile on the left and turn right, with the hedge to the right. The motorway is parallel not many metres away. The path goes through a small copse and then drops sharply into the small valley below. The motorway is high up to the left. Go leftwards towards the stile by the tunnel under the

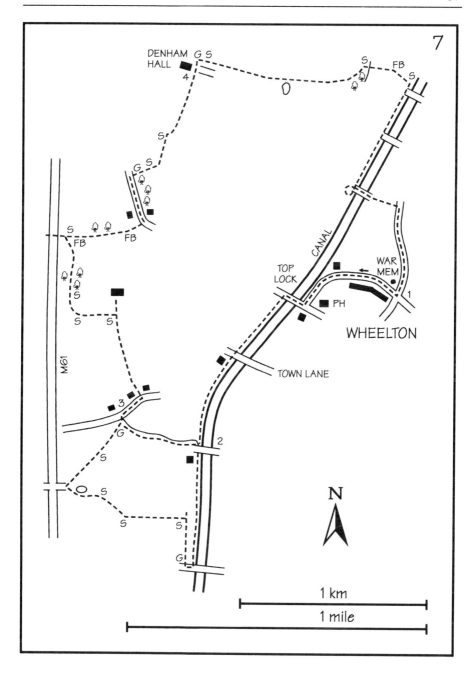

motorway. Over it, if there is time, go through the long gloomy tunnel. At the end of it, the path then continues by the river as it goes through another tunnel. It is an interesting experience.

Returning to the footbridge go over it. Turn right over the stile and follow the edge of the stream through the field. A landscaped path then goes through a stretch of woodland by the river. Emerging in the open, make for the footbridge ahead. Over it, turn left over the stile. Go across the field in the direction the stile is facing, with the river going away to the left towards the houses on the bank. Aim to the right of the small groups of trees. Go over the stile and up a short wooded path o the road, by the footpath sign.

Turn left along he road, over the bridge and through the houses, with Riverside and Brookside on the left. The road ascends through woodland, with the stream appearing and disappearing on the right. On the same side, is a low green fence. Just after the woodland ends, turn right at a footpath sign, over the small stream and through the gate. Follow the wide track uphill, through the middle of the field. At the next gate, go over the stile alongside it. Continue ahead, until reaching another gate. Do not go over it, but turn left along the edge of the field, to a gate by a stile. Then follow the track which goes right and then ahead along the left side of the hedge. Denham Hall farm is ahead. As the farm is reached at a gate, continue ahead to the right of the house. Pass a track coming in from the left and a shed and lane on the right.

4. At the gate facing you, go over the wall stile on its right. Bear right across the large field towards the right-hand corner. Do not take the stile further to the left, nearer to Walmsley Fold Farm. The proper right of way continues to the left of the pond in the field to the right. The County Council has promised to ensure that stiles are erected in the fence. Otherwise, go through the gate just to the left of the right-hand corner. Then turn right, passing a gate on the right and coming quickly to another gate ahead. Do not go through it, but turn left, keeping to the fence. Going downhill, eventually there is a gully on the right. Pass a stile and follow the fence as it bears to the left at the bottom of the field, with a steep tree clad bank on the right.

At the stile in the fence, turn right and, descending the bank, bear left towards the stepping stones across the stream. Go right across the field towards the footbridge. Go forward and up the steep bank to a stile hidden in the trees, just to the left of the bridge. At the canal, turn right under the bridge, along the towpath. On the left are moorings for barges. Pass under another bridge. The canal then bends to a third. Immediately after passing under it, take the stile on the right. The wide track swings back across the bridge and then ascends upwards with hedges on both sides. Go over an unusual stile and turn right along the road. There is a good view of the canal down in the valley. Go through barriers as the road narrows for a short stretch to prevent it being a through road for traffic. After a second set of barriers the road widens again and soon you are back in the village centre.

8. Chorley

A figure of eight walk close to Chorley and Coppull, taking in part of the Yarrow Valley Park and Duxbury Park.

Route: Birkacre – Burgh Hall – Duxbury Woods – Yarrow Valley Park – Birkacre.

Start: Yarrow Valley Park car park. Grid reference: 470 153

Distance: 6 miles.

Duration: 3 hours.

Map: SD 41/51.

By car: Situated between Chorley and Coppull, Yarrow Valley Park is signposted off the road at grid reference 569 157, although the Birkacre Garden Centre sign will be more observable. Pass the Garden Centre and the car park is to the left, just before the bridge.

Refreshments: Yarrow Bridge Inn and Hop Pocket.

---

1. From the car park, go back to the road, with the bridge to your left. Turn sharply right up a wide track, which, at first, has low railings on the left. As the track ascends, it swings sharply to the right, with Highbank House ahead of you. Do not take the turning to the left, but go straight on, passing two houses to your left. To your right is woodland and, down beyond, the lake. Pass the stiles to your left and right. Follow the track round to the left, with a house on the corner. As the track goes gently uphill, there is a hedge to the right, with a field between it and the woodland. There is open land to the left.

The track levels out. After passing a few trees and a gate on the left, continue on past the cottage, which has a footpath gate just beyond it. With trees to the right, the lane comes to the private entrance of Burgh Hall. Just before the entrance, go left onto the road. Turn right up to the roundabout, with Fir Tree Lane opposite. Turn right again and when faced by the barriers to an unused road, turn left by the sign for Yew

Tree Close and Burg Lane South. After a few metres, with Yew Tree Close to the left, turn right down the wide track. As the line of trees in the hedge on the right come to an end, there is a stile on the left, by a lone tree and old gate.

2. [A small extension to the walk at this point is to continue along the lane for a short distance. At the division of ways, take the lane to the left, with a gate which is usually open. There is a single wire fence on either side. Pass the farm access road on the right, with its private notice. Continue on down the lane, with a hedge to the left. Reaching a house to the left, continue along in front of it to a stile. Cross a very small field to another stile ahead at the entrance to the woodland. Over the stile, do not follow the path downwards, but turn left. Follow the path along the edge of the wood. Soon the path bends to the right and arrives just below another stile. Here join the shorter route].

Cross the stile and walk with the hedge to the right. Pass under the telegraph wires. Just after some trees along the hedge, go over the stile in the wire fence ahead. Continue downhill with the fence now on the left. At the end of the fence and after a stone indicating a footpath, continue across the centre of the field towards the woodland, with a house over to the right. At a stile by another stone footpath indicator, go down the wooden steps into the woodland.

When the path comes to a T Junction by the river, turn left. From here, the path follows the river through Duxbury Woods for about a mile. Along the way, there is one short downward slope, a bend in the river with a little beach alongside a wooden walkway for when the water is running at its height and a small plank walk. Otherwise there are few landmarks. Whenever the path seems to split, it joins again within a short distance.

Eventually, soon after passing a path that goes off to the left, you arrive at a footbridge over the river. On the other side, follow the path to the left, ignoring one immediately to the right. It moves away from the river and emerges, through rhododendrons, into the open.

3. Although there is a metal road that comes in a semi-circle ahead, turn left along the one that has rhododendron bushes to the right and trees to the left. The pathway then goes across the centre of park-land, interspersed with trees. It eventually comes to the A6 by the lodge entrance. But, to avoid walking along the A6, go left from the pathway towards the edge of the trees. Here take the dirt track that continues along the edge of the river, which is in the valley below. After the weir in the river, the path continues through scrubland, until it emerges on the A6 to the left of a bush-shelter. The Yarrow Bridge Inn is on the opposite side of the road.

Cross the bridge and turn immediately left along the railings, with houses on the right. As another road comes in from the right, Plessey's factory is on the left. Pass the lane on the left and continue to turn left into Little Carr Lane. The Hop Pocket Inn is on the other side of the road.

At the end of Little Carr Lane is the entrance to the Norweb Training Centre. There is a notice of no public access except for the right of way. Walk straight ahead along the road, passing various numbered car parks and keeping the main building to the right. Just beyond the electricity sub-station on the left, go ahead along the wide grass track. As the fencing on the right ends, do not continue on the track that descends ahead, but turn sharply right along a path through the trees. After going over the bed of a stream, the path goes up sharply to the right, passing a large beech tree at the top of the rise. At the split of paths, take the one to the right and in a short distance come to the edge of a school playing field.

Go at an angle of 45° to the left across the playing field, away from the school buildings. In the wooden fence, lined with trees, is a stile. Over this, cross the centre of the field, aiming for the pole ahead. Beyond the pole, slightly to the right, is a stile in the hedge, with a footpath sign.

4. Turn left along the lane, passing a road to the left and an estate path to the right. After the white cottage on the left, go through the bollards onto the road. Cross the road. Go through the

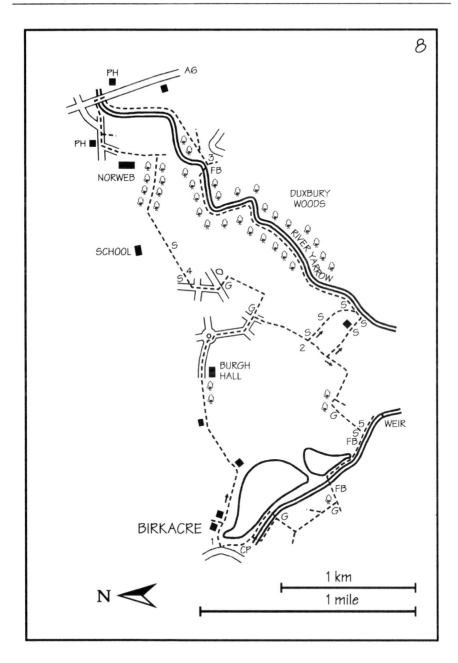

green gate and past the seats and pond on the left. The path goes between the woodland on the left and the fences of the houses on the right. Soon it turns to the right and continues between woods and houses. At the end of the fences on the right, turn right. Pass a path coming in from the left and a pond on the right. Go through the gate and emerge at the earlier point on the walk by Yew Tree Close.

Turn left along the lane previously walked until reaching the split of ways. Take the lane descending to the right. A pond will be seen in the field to the right and a farm across to the left. The lane turns sharply to the right and, after a dip, sharply again to the left. Instead of following the lane to the left, go straight ahead into a small copse. In a few metres you are at a gate, with an old stone marking a gap on its left. Do not take the path that goes way to the left, but carry straight on down hill. There are excellent views across the valley ahead. The path reaches a stile at the bottom of the hill by the river.

5. If there is time, turn left along the path for a short way to see the small weir. Otherwise turn right over the lake overflow bridge and continue, with the river on the left. After the gate across the path, go over the sturdy bridge on the left, opposite the small lake. From the bridge, the path starts to go uphill. After a few metres, you come to a gate in the trees on the right. Go through the smaller gate by the side of it. The track goes through a short section of trees and then into open ground. Pass a path going to the right. As the track bends to the left, take one going at an angle to the right. As this descends, it is joined by another coming in from the right. At the bottom of the hill, there is a choice of ways for the last short section.

The first is to continue along the wide track ahead. The second is to go through the gate on the right, cross the river and take the short flight of steps to the left onto the edge of the lake. Then go left and, near to the end of the lake, take the steps back down to the track. You emerge just beyond the point where the stream comes back under the main track.

From here, turn right, go through the gate and arrive back at the car park.

Lake in Yarrow Valley Park

9. Anglezarke

The fledgling River Yarrow, the silence of the moorland, ruined cottages and an old lead mine, all in the shadow of Winter Hill, feature in this valley walk.

Route: Yarrow Reservoir – Dean Wood – The Hempshaws – Yarrow Reservoir.

Start: There are a few parking spaces by the reservoir bridge at grid reference 627 160. On busy summer week-ends, it may be necessary to park in the Anglezarke car park, grid reference 621 161. From this car park, with Moor Road going uphill to the left, walk towards the triangle. As Knowsley Lane goes to the right, take Parson's Bullough Road to the left, the signpost pointing to Rivington and Belmont. Join the walk at point 2.

Distance: 4½ miles.

Duration: 2½ hours.

Map: SD 61/71

By car: From the traffic lights in the centre of Adlington, turn along Babylon Lane. At the Bay Horse Inn, turn right. Almost immediately cross the motorway and turn let along the road marked Anglezarke. Pass the Yew Tree Inn on the right. At the triangle, turn right towards Rivington and Belmont to reach the reservoir bridge, or left to the Anglezarke car park.

Refreshments: Bay Horse Inn and Yew Tree Inn.

1. From the bridge walk west along the road, by the edge of the reservoir, until reaching a concessionary bridle way sign by a gate on the left.

2. Follow the wide path, with a wall on both sides. Pass steps going down to the reservoir to the left and a small tower shaped building on the right. From this point there are trees on either side. Cross a bridge and continue on as the track descends. After passing a path coming in from the right and the higher ground to the left, the track becomes a country lane through open ground. Rivington Pike can be seen in the distance over to the left.

Arriving at the gate at the end of the lane, turn left. Do not follow the waymark to the right. As the track bends to the right through the trees, do not take the track to the left.

Soon, at the level bridge, you will meet a path coming in on the right, from the far side of the stream. Go through the waymarked access gate ahead. The stream is now to your left. Walk on through the avenue of trees and over the flat stone wall bridge. After a stone wall, with an unused door in it on the right, the track goes right towards Delph Wood House.

As it does so, bear left at 45° (not through the gate to the left) and follow the path the short distance up to a stile. Do not follow the path ahead, but turn right, gently ascending along the edge of the fenced wood. After a Nature Reserve notice and couple of large stones, come to a stile in a wooden fence at the end of the field. Looking back fine views can be seen.

Going right over the stile, with another nature reserve notice on the right, follow the enclosed path on the left, along the edge of the deep wooded valley. The path has a stone base for the first few metres. After a stone wall to the left, the path continues through an avenue of trees. Going under the bough of a tree low over the path, follow the fence round to the right to come to the road by a gate.

3. Turn left along the road. By a 'Slow, Farm entrance' sign, it bends to the right towards Wilcock's Farm. The year 1670 can be seen on the front of the farm house. As the road bends left towards the house, find a ladder stile, by a pole, on the right. Cross the small field, with a farm shed on the left, towards two trees in the opposite corner. Go left over the ladder stile, just before the trees.

The path goes along the left edge of the stream. Having gone by the small paddock railings to the left after the stile, you are in a large field. There are intermittent trees on the far side of the stream. A ruined wall then runs along the path side. After this, cross a waymarked stile in a wire fence. The path crosses a tiny side stream and then goes between the edge of the stream and the gully.

Cross another small side stream, immediately before the next stile. Keep to the right of the fence. At a waymarker on a post, a stone wall begins. It is wise to follow the path a couple of metres away from the wall, especially when conditions are wet. You are now almost in the shadow of Winter Hill, with its mast.

Cross the stile going over the wall to the left. If the gate immediately ahead is open go through it. Otherwise use the stile in the fence to its left to cross onto the track ahead. Keep the fence on the left. Pass an old wooden bridge across the gully on the right and a pond on the left. As you gradually ascend, you will pass a fir plantation on the left and a stone wall coming in from the right. At the waymark on a post to not take the path branching right, but keep to the one along the fence. There are the ruins of an old sheep dip on the left. Ahead, at the stone wall, is a three-way sign post. Note that the next section needs a little care in navigating, since there are so many paths, including ones made by the sheep.

4. Turn right along the wall, passing the gateway. Follow the track that bends slowly right uphill towards the waymarker post. Do not take the path going off downhill to the left. At the waymarker, continue uphill bearing to the left. The path can be a little faint at this stage. Make sure that you remain parallel to the stone wall a little higher up.

In a few minutes, as another wall comes across, you will see a waymarker post. Continue ahead, closer to the parallel wall. Pass a ruined cottage and a wooden gatepost. A few metres on, there is another waymarker post. Still keep ahead to reach a junction of paths by a signpost. Here turn left along the wall and quickly right through the gap by a post with a waymarker on it. The path, with a small valley to the left, drops down to a stone bridge over the stream.

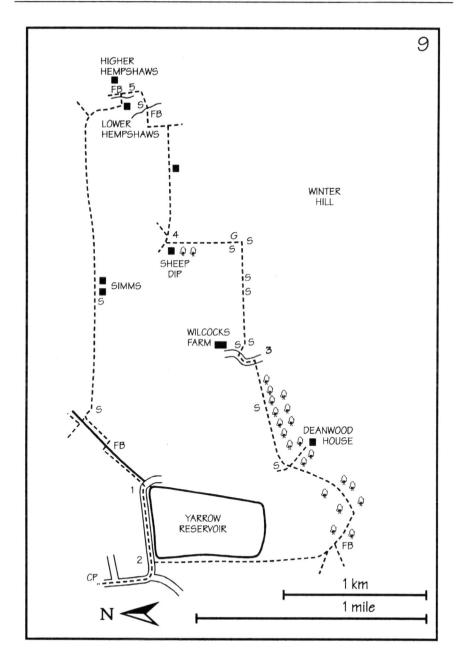

Higher Hempshaws old farm

On the other side, go over the stile by the map of the area and directly uphill for a minute or so. The ground levels out, as the track keeps to the right of a wall and then goes left through a gap in it. This leads across open land to a deserted cottage, Higher Hempshaws. Follow the track, over the stream, and to the left uphill to the ruins of Lower Hempshaws.

5. The track bears sharply right by the ruins and continues with a wall to the left and a wire fence on the right. You are now out in moorland, with Sam Pasture rising to the right. The track now bends sharply left over a small stream. Ignore the path going uphill to the right. From here you are going down the opposite side of the valley from the one you came up. There is gully to the right, then a small stream to cross, and a gully again. The track bears right uphill for a little and then left to descend past a little quarry on the right. There are some small fir plantations higher up the slope. You come to the ruined cottages of Simms, beyond which is a stile. The way then goes on, passing a number of streams and old walls.

Eventually another stile is reached. Over it the track quickly descends to the stream in a reverse half circle. At the stream do not take the road going up the hill, but turn left, keeping the stream to the right.

You will come to a notice board with a map. This explains that you are in the Lead Mines Clough area. The mines commenced in the 1690s, were at their peak in the 1780s and closed in 1837. The remains of the waterwheel pit, the top of a shaft and a lime pit can still be seen. The map indicates the position of each.

From the notice board, cross the footbridge over the stream. Follow the track with the wall above the stream on the left and passing a quarry on the right. At the gate, by the bridleway sign, arrive back at the bridge.

10. Worthington Lakes

This walk includes the lakes at Worthington and the surrounding countryside. There is one, short, moderate uphill section.

Route: Worthington Lakes – Canal – Arley Hall – Worthington Lanes.

Start: Worthington Lakes Visitor Centre. Grid reference: 581 105.

Distance: 5 or 4½ miles.

Duration: 2½ or 2 hours.

Map: SD 41/51.

By car: The Lakes Centre is a right turn on the A5106 shortly north of the junction of the B5239 from Standish. The turn is not obvious. The signpost, which is on the left side of the road, is small and tends to be obscured in the hedge. Park in the upper car-park by the centre. Toilet facilities are available.

Refreshments: Kilhey Court Hotel, which is a little further north on the main road beyond the Lakes entrance.

---

1. Take the path to the right of the visitor centre and follow it as it slopes down towards the lake. At the lakeside, turn left along the level path that runs through the trees, alongside the edge of the lake. At the end of Worthington Lake do not turn right on the path that runs between it and Arley Lake, but continue along the left edge of Arley Lake. The path is now more winding and up and down. There are fields to the left.

At the end of Arley Lake, go over the small bridge. Again do not follow the path between the lakes, but keep to the left, along the side of the inlet stream. Immediately after crossing a footbridge, turn right, between railings, to another foot-bridge across Adlington lake. The path swings to the right and then left again. Do not take the path ahead, but turn right along the east edge of the lake.

2. At first there are railings on the lakeside and fields to the left.

Lake at Worthington

After going over a short stretch of boarding and passing a clump of trees to the left, go over a stile. Ignore the path to the right. Go straight ahead towards Arley Wood. Go over the stile and take the path, with railings on the right, into the wood. With other paths coming in from the left, the track drops down towards the River Douglas. At one point you pass over some steeping stones laid along the path.

At the river, turn right and cross over the railed bridge. Carry on ahead up the hill. At the cross road of paths turn left and continue the steady ascent, passing a path coming in from the left. The track gradually bears right through the trees to reach the towpath of the Leeds – Liverpool canal. Go left along the towpath. The wood continues to the left and is then replaced by a view of the Douglas Valley.

3. There is a choice of routes:

Shorter Walk:

After passing a large house on the opposite bank, reach the

first canal bridge, turn left just before it, turn right up the short path and then right over the bridge. After a short distance, the disused railtrack crosses the lane. The longer walk links at this point.

Longer Walk:

Continue along the towpath to the second (Aberdeen) bridge. Access to it is on the far side. Cross the bridge, go through the gap at the side of the gate and, with a line of trees to the left, aim for the gate on the opposite side of the field. Through the gate, go right, through another gate, onto the disused railtrack. There are high hedges on either side. A farm road runs parallel with it on the left. At the junction, where it is crossed by another track by a number of gates, continue ahead. The next junction of tracks is where the shorter walk comes in from the right.

Walk left up the wide farm track towards Aberdeen Farm. Go through the white gate ahead. Then, opposite to the farm house, turn right through another white gate. You are now on another wide farm track. This is at first a metal surface and then dirt. There is a high hedge to the right and telegraph poles to the left. Just after the track is lined with trees on both sides, it joins another one coming from the left. Turn right and, with Hollins Head Farm to the left, go at right angles along the narrow metal road. On reaching a small cluster of houses the track becomes a dirt one again. Carry straight on, passing by, on the left, a house adjacent to a bridge over the old railway. Then after some old farm sheds on the right and Abbey Farm on the left, the canal bridge is crossed.

4. Follow the track round to the right, through the car barrier and pass Arley Hall to the right. This is the home of Wigan Golf Club. Continue on the track as it gradually slopes down, through the golf course, until reaching the woods. Just after a hedge begins on the left, take the path that goes right into the woods. Follow this down until reaching the bridge over the River Douglas, which you crossed earlier in the walk. Turn left along the path until reaching the stile.

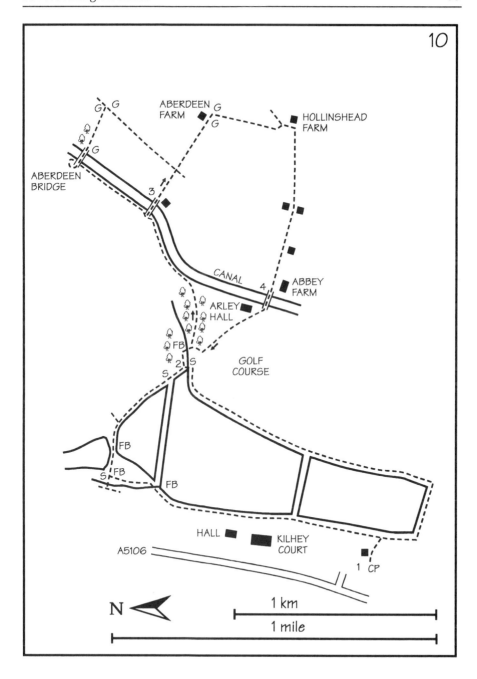

Take the path to the left, along the wooden railings. A notice warns of exposed tree roots, which are found a bit later along the way. Coming to an information board on the left, go straight on along the edge of the lake. There are railings on the right of the path. At the end of the path, turn right along the southern end of the lake. At the 'Private Road' notice turn right and soon after left back to the Visitors Centre.

11. Haigh Country Park

*Haigh Hall and its country park are the scene of this walk
through fields and woodland.*

Route: Haigh Hall – Haigh Plantations – Haigh Village – Haigh Hall

Start: Haigh Hall, Wigan. Grid reference: 597 088.

Distance: 6 miles.

Duration: 3 hours.

Maps: SD 40/50 and SD 60/70

Car: There are car entrances to Haigh Hall from the B5239 just on the
                  Haigh side of Red Rock (Grid Reference: 592 095) and Haigh
                  Village (Grid reference: 607 090) and on the B5238 along Higher
                  Lane (Grid reference: 606 076). There are two car parks
                  immediately adjacent to the Hall. A small parking fee is charged.

Refreshments: Café at Haigh Hall (open every day except Mondays in winter),
                  Colliers Arms, near Higher Lane and Balcarres Arms in Haigh
                  Village.

1. There has been a Hall at Haigh for many centuries. The word
Haigh means 'enclosure' and originally was simply a clearing
in the forest. The present Hall, now a conference centre, was
built between 1830 and 1849. It was bought by Wigan Corporation in 1947 and in recent years has been much developed
by the Leisure Department. It now boasts a golf course, children's playground, model village, crazy golf, a miniature
railway, cafeteria and shop, plus woodland walks in all of 125
acres. A short history of Haigh Hall by Godfrey Talbot can be
bought in the Information Centre.

From the car parks set out in a north-westerly direction along
the metalled road, which is one of the car entrances to the
Hall. As with all the access roads, there are 'sleeping police-
men' along the way. After passing part of the golf course on
the left, there are good views across to Winter Hill over to the

right. Pass a copse, with a track running through it, to the left and then another clump of woodland with a disused quarry on the right. Coming to a large house on the right with a footpath sign pointing through its grounds, follow instead the sign to the left of the road.

You are now on a wide stony path, which gradually starts to descend towards the canal. To the left is a house with a high fir hedge and then a cluster of renovated buildings. Come to the canal bridge, with Pendlebury House on the right. Pass through the gate across the track and over the bridge. The track, with wire fences and hedges on either side, passes a small farm on the right and then a line of houses on the same side.

With a house opposite, follow the track to the left with Samuel Fold Cottage on the left corner. Go on through the woods and under a demolished bridge. The track bends to the left under another old railway bridge, this time not demolished. There are now fields to the left and woodland on the right. Eventually, there are some small factories on the right.

Arriving at the end of Pendlebury Lane, you are now on a metal road. Down to the right, in the valley, is the River Douglas. The road follows it for the next few minutes. There is wire fencing on the right and trees on the left. After passing the entrance to Wigan Rugby Football Club to the left, there is woodland on both sides of the road. Next there is a line of houses on the left, behind some fine beech trees. At the end of some unsightly tin fencing on the right, come to a T-junction.

2. To the right can be seen the river bridge. The route is to the left, starting to go uphill. A Douglas Valley Way sign will be seen. Do not continue up the road as it bends to the right, but go up the stone path on the right, which ascends to a seat, where it rejoins the road.

From Haigh Brow Cottage on the left, there are houses on both sides of the road for a while. Then there are fields on either side, until you soon reach a bridge over a disused railway. On

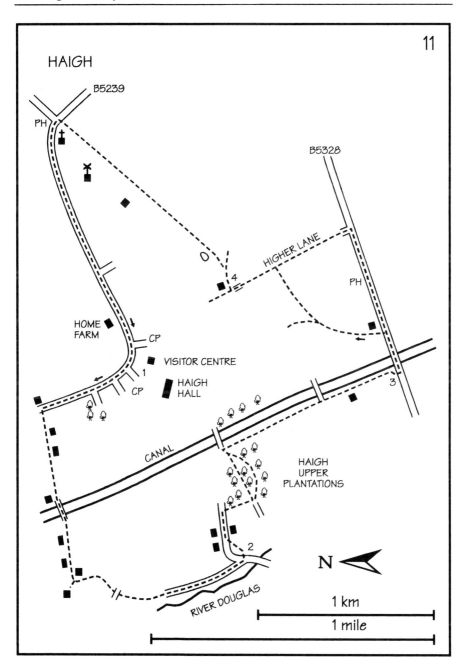

11

HAIGH

B5239

PH

B5328

HIGHER LANE

PH

D

4

HOME
FARM

CP

VISITOR CENTRE

1

HAIGH
HALL

CP

3

CANAL

HAIGH
UPPER
PLANTATIONS

2

N

RIVER DOUGLAS

1 km

1 mile

the far side of the bridge turn right. The path goes along the edge of the embankment. It is possible to walk on the old track bed, but this can at times be somewhat muddy.

After a short distance, the narrow embankment path comes onto a much wider path. (If you are on the track bed path, move back up the embankment after a few hundred metres). Continue, parallel to the railway, on this wider path, through High Upper Plantations, ignoring all paths going to the left. You will come to a metal road crossing at right angles. Turn right and, immediately before the ornamental bridge over the track, go left.

Follow the path as it winds its way through the woods, until reaching another narrow metalled road. Here, turn right to the nearby canal bridge. On the nearside of the bridge, go down the steps on the right. Walk along the towpath. First there is woodland on both sides and then fields on the right. Pass a milepost stating 'Leeds 89¾ – Liverpool 38'. Continue on under another bridge. After a ruined farm on the right, a track can be seen running parallel to the towpath.

3. Go onto this track until it reaches the road. Turn left back across the canal bridge. There is a choice of way here:

Either:

If a visit to the Colliers Arms is required, continue up the left-hand side of the road until the pub is reached. Upon leaving continue up the road and turn left into Higher Lane, opposite to Ivy Mount. A sign indicates the Country Park. This lane is another car access to Haigh Hall. Walk along it, passing houses on the right.

Or:

After crossing the canal bridge, turn left along the lane in front of the house. There is no footpath sign. The lane goes through open land. Over to the left is a house with a rotunda on the roof. After a while, there is a clump of trees on the right, at the bottom of a slope. Go down the slope and cross over the wooden footbridge. The path is narrow and follows, in a small culvert, the left-hand side of a field. Later there are bushes on both sides of the path. It emerges onto Higher Lane, where turn left. Note that the path can be overgrown in summer. Walk left along Higher Lane, until reaching the disused railway bridge.

4. Over the bridge, turn right and follow the path, with the grounds of a house to the left and trees to the right. At the end of the hedge on the left, turn left as the main path goes on. The path now runs through an avenue of trees. Pass by a pond on the left. Prospect Cottages can be seen across the fields to the left. On this same side there is eventually woodland to the left along the path. There are logs across the path at various stages. The path becomes a much wider one on reaching a track coming in from the left. Across to the right the row of houses comes nearer. After passing the graveyard on the left, the path reaches Haigh Village, by the Balcarres Arms.

Turn left along the front of the church and go by the school

Windmill at Haigh Hall

on the right. The metal road continues, with some houses on the right side. In a field to the left, is a windmill. Eventually there is a stone wall to the left, enclosing woods. Pass a turning to the left and Home Farm on the right, to arrive back at the car parks.

12. Aspull

A trip to America is not often included in books of walks. This one is able to transport you right across the world in no time at all.

Route: Aspull Village – Hindley Hall – America Wood – Borsdane Wood – Aspull Village.

Start: Civic Hall car Park, Aspull. Grid reference 613 077.

Distance: 5 miles.

Duration: 2½ hours.

Map: SD 60/70

By car: From the crossroads of the B5238 and B5239 at Aspull, take the road towards Wigan. After passing Crawford Street on the left, take the next turn left into Woods Road. There is a bridle path sign pointing along it, plus signs for the Civic Hall and Aspull Rugby Club. A few hundred metres down the road, there is a large car park on the left.

Refreshments: The Running Horses.

---

1. From the car park, with the Civic Hall opposite, turn left and walk further along the lane. After two old gate posts, come to a cottage on the left. At the fork of path, take the one to the right, which leads towards the back of the Rugby Club grounds. There is open ground to the right. At the car barrier, carry on along the path, with a gully and trees on the left and a low fence on the right. After passing a number of paths coming in from the right, soon after a stile on the right, turn left down steps to a bridge across the stream. On the other side follow the wide path across the open field. It goes on through woodland, passing over a stream. At a T-junction of paths turn right. The woods are now on your right and fields on the left. The path drops down, in an open space, to a stream and then climbs up steps a short distance into the woods.

Immediately in the woods, turn left along the wide path through the trees. Again, pass various paths coming in from the right. Eventually, the trees come to an end and there is a fence on both sides. After a gate and old stone on the left, and with poles coming in from the left, arrive at a car barrier. Cross Withington Lane.

Go ahead on the track with the low pailing across it. There is a fence to the left and open land, with factories in the distance to the right. At the T-junction of paths, turn left. There is now a tall wire mesh fence around the land fill site on the right. On the left is a wood and a wire fence, followed by just a wire fence. Next, on the left, are some trees, behind which is the golf course.

Just after a tree actually on the path, turn at right angles. The wire mesh fence is still on the right, with a wooden one to the left. The path is some distance above the ground to the left. At the end of the path, turn left down a flight of railed steps. Turn right along the track. Do not follow one which soon goes off to the right. Continue ahead, passing the farm yard of Bank House to your left. The ground opens up again on the right. The path follows a line of trees.

2. Turn left, as the main track continues on, onto a wide path. There is a small new plantation on the right, a fence and occasional trees on the left. An another T-junction, turn left, with the golf course and the Power Packing Export Services works ahead of you.

This is a narrower dirt path, with a fence on the left and first, a hedge, and then trees to the right. At the end of the path, go straight on to a farm track, coming from a gate on the left. Pass the back of the farm buildings and an old gatepost. There is a bungalow on the left. The track swings right in front of it. You can now see Hindley Hall, the headquarters of the golf club, on the right and the lakes away to the left.

Continue along the metal track, until it reaches the road. Turn right and, just before the first house on the left, turn down a narrow path. This passes along the side of the house and

Hindley Hall

garden, then goes into the trees. Coming out of them, do not aim for the gate to the right, but follow the path along the right edge of a gully.

Soon the gully becomes a deep one, full of trees. There is a single line of trees to the right of the path. Then it begins to descend into open ground. At the bottom of the incline, a wide path crosses. This is now America Wood.

3. Turn left and it is now simply a matter of following the path through the woods, with the stream to the right. Keep on the track for mile. You will pass two wooden footbridges crossing the stream. Then you will come to a bridge with iron railings. The steps coming down to it on the far side of the stream are steep and straight.

Do not cross the bridge, but turn up the path to the left, opposite the bridge. A steep short climb to the left brings you to an old wooden stile. Go on along the path across the field, running parallel to the poles. This passes to the right of the garden and back of a cottage. Go straight on down Bagshaw Lane, passing a white cottage and barn to the left. The lane runs between hedges, with poles on both sides. There is grass in the middle of the lane.

4. On reaching the cluster of houses at Pennington Green, turn right, just before the first house on the right. This is just after a double wooden fence on the right. There is no signpost, but go to the right of the gate and up the track which has a fence on the left. Further along the track come to another gate and go through the gap at the left of it. There is now a low hedge on the left. As you reach the end of the lane, there is a small gate to the left of it. This takes you along a path, fenced on both sides, around the side of the farm.

The path reaches the wall of the reservoir, with the track to the farm coming in from the right. Join this track, for the few metres until the T-junction. Turn left along the track along the front of the reservoir. As it goes away to the right, turn left, with the stone wall on your left, towards the entrance gate to a cottage. The sign, Aspull Reservoir, is on the gateway. To the right of it is a gate and a wicket gate with the water board notice, public pathway. Go down the concrete path and then turn towards another gate to the right.

Go through the wicket gate and keep the hedge to the right. Then the path runs across a field, between wire fences, leading onto a wider track. Keep straight ahead, with a wire fence to the right, to arrive at a road. Cross onto the pavement on the other side of the road. Quickly turn right by a gate, onto a farm track. Follow this, with the hedge to the right. Do not take the track going off to the left, but carry on. The track is crossed by telegraph wires.

After a small plantation to the right, come to a gate. Pass to the right of it. For a few metres, the path is between wire fences, but then there is just the fence on the left. Carry straight on, as a wider track comes in from the right. At the end of the fence, by an old gatepost, another track comes in, this time from the left. Keep on across the open ground. The rugby ground can be seen to the left. Soon you will arrive at a cottage. Follow the track past the cottage, back to the car park.

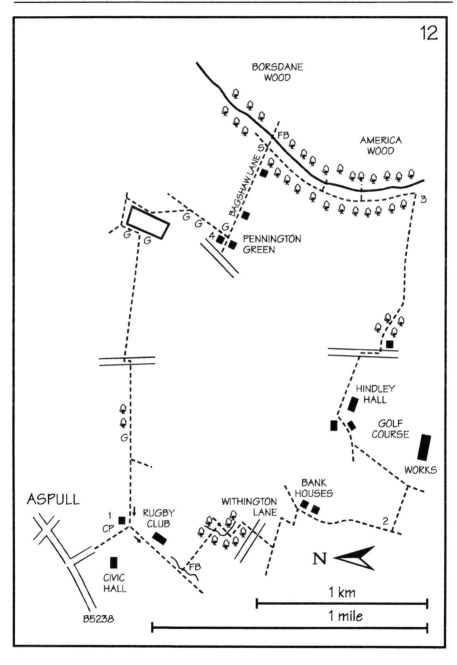

12

BORSDANE WOOD

AMERICA WOOD

FB

BAGSHAW LANE S

G G

G G G

4 PENNINGTON GREEN

3

HINDLEY HALL

GOLF COURSE

WORKS

G

ASPULL

1 CP

RUGBY CLUB

WITHINGTON LANE

BANK HOUSES

2

CIVIC HALL

FB

N

1 km

1 mile

B5238

13. Pennington Flash

Much of the area in which this walk takes place has been reclaimed and landscaped by the Wigan Local Authority to form a pleasant recreational area surrounding the lake of Pennington Flash.

Route: Lift Bridge – Visitor Centre – Sorrowcow Farm – Mossley Hall Farm – Lift Bridge.

Start: The car park at the canal lift bridge. Grid reference: 631 997.

Distance: 3¾ miles.

Duration: 2 hours.

Map: SJ 69/79.

By car: From the A580 East Lancs Road, take the A572 road northwards, following the Pennington Flash brown signs. For the lift bridge, turn left at the traffic lights and later right into Sandy Lane, opposite the Church. Follow the road around until coming to a T-junction. Turn right to the lift bridge.

Refreshments: The main Flash car park usually has a refreshment van during the summer months. Information and toilets are at the adjacent Visitor Centre.

***

1. From the lift bridge, walk along the tow path to the right, going under the telegraph wires and past the turning place. Winter Hill can be seen in the distance over to the left. After the canal narrows, there is a small valley to the left. Passing a black and white coloured manhole, there is a good view of the Flash over to the right.

Reach a bridge over the canal, which leads over towards houses on the other side. Here there is a choice of ways:

Either:

Turn right down the steps. A sand path can be seen going left after a few metres, which you take.

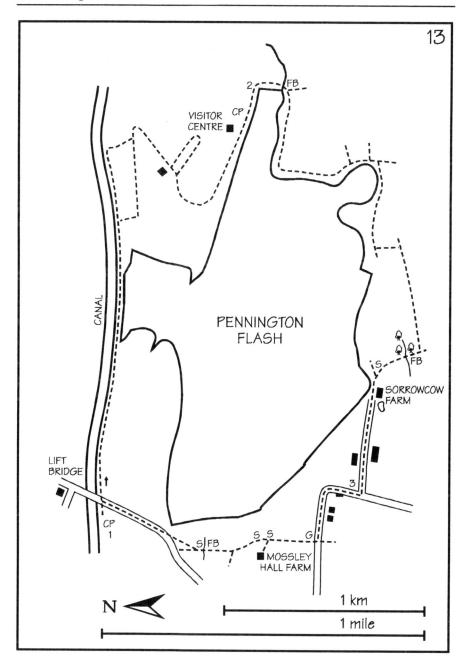

Or:

Continue along the tow path, until reaching wooden steps which descend down the bank to a parallel track. From this, more steps will take you down to cross another track. Follow the grass track, until it meets the sand one coming in from the right.

The path winds for a little way. The golf course will then become visible over to the left. Do not take the grass track straight ahead, but keep on the sand track as it bends to the right, with a stream and hedge to the right. Ignore all paths coming in from the right, until you reach Lapwing Hide. Here turn left across the grass track, until reaching a track from the left, by the golf course. Turn right and then sharp right again. This will bring you on to a wide tree shaded track.

At the end of the track, turn left back onto the sand track again. This takes you towards the lake, with trees along the edge of it. Soon you are by the lake-side. Follow the path along the edge of the lake, until reaching the Visitors Centre and car park.

2. From the car park, go left along the edge of the lake. Then the solid path goes along the side of trees and a fence for a short while, until coming to a footbridge over the feeder stream. A little way back upstream is the bridge of the old railway, now turned into a road. Over the bridge turn right and as the main path goes ahead turn quickly right along the edge of the stream. Soon the path is following the edge of the lake, with open ground to the left. The car park you have left can be seen across the other side of the water. Pass the short path to East Bay Hide on the right. Pass two paths coming in from the left from a parallel one a few metres away. Keep on past the seat. Leave the path ahead, to turn right through a small gate to a path which continues with the lake to the right. It goes through trees and bushes.

Take the next path to the left as it goes upwards top join another one coming in from the left. Turn right and follow it through a small copse until reaching a T-junction. Opposite is another small copse. Here turn right. Go over a footbridge. There is woodland on the right and a field to the left. Next there is a small chicane to negotiate. A little later come to a stile by a notice warning to keep dogs on a lead.

There are iron railings on the right and the end of which is a written footpath notice. With a wide track coming in from the right, pass the houses and sheds of Sorrowcow Farm on the left. The track becomes a metal road. After the pond on the left, there is a row of neat little cottages. To the right is the yacht marina. At the end of the road, which is Green Lane, turn right at the T-junction and join the pavement on the far side. Just after the 40 mph sign, the road bends sharply left.

3. After two houses on the left come to a track coming in from the left and continuing on the other side of the road, by a footpath sign. Follow the direction of the sign, being careful to shut the gate behind you as requested. The fenced track gradually slopes downwards. There are trees in the field to the right.

Lift Bridge

As the track bends left into Mossley Hall Farm, look for a big wooden stile on the right. Over it, keep close to the brick wall. Go on through the small copse to another stile. The path now runs alongside a hedge. After passing a track going left, the path continues ahead, with a wire fence on the left and a row of bushes on the right.

Cross the flat stone bridge over the stream by a stile. Pass under the telegraph wires through open ground. As the path continues to a stile onto the road just ahead, take the path to the right, which brings you onto the road a little further to the right. You are now on the A578, which can be quite busy. After going by a small car-park and the road to the land reclamation site, follow the short path with railings, up to the lift bridge onto the Leigh branch of the Leeds – Liverpool canal.

14. Carr Mill Dam

A stroll, on the edge of St Helens, around Carr Mill Dam and its surrounding countryside.

Route: Car Mill Dam – Startham Hall – Holin Hey Farm – Carr Mill Dam.

Start: The Waterside Inn, Carr Mill. Grid reference: 523 975

Distance: 4½ or 3½ miles.

Duration: 2 or 1½ hours.

Map: SJ 49/59

By car: From the A580 East Lancashire Road turn onto the A571. Immediately turn right into Old Garswood Road, bear right round the Waterside Inn and park on the left by the lakeside.

Refreshments: Waterside Inn at Carr Mill and Masons Arms at Chadwick Green.

---

1. From the car, walk left along the edge of the lake. The path goes past the back of the inn. Note for arriving back, that refreshments can be taken on the veranda, which gives a good view out over the lake. Follow on through the trees at the edge of the lake. The volume of walkers has meant that there are now three well worn paths parallel to each other, so choose whichever you prefer. At the beginning the way stays fairly close to the road, but soon there are fields to the left.

Eventually in the distance you will see the viaduct of 19 arches which crosses the lake. It carries water from the Reservoir at Rivington to Liverpool. The lake or dam itself was created in the eighteenth century to supply water to the Sankey Navigation. The outlet can be seen towards the end of the walk. After passing to the left of the viaduct, the path quickly arrives at a very wide gravel lane. Turn right, passing a smaller lake on the left. Arriving at Otter's Swift Farm, turn right. (The main track continues ahead, through a gate). There is now a fence on the right and a ditch to the left.

The track swings sharply to the left. The farmer's footpath sign

Carr Mill Lake

points the way. At Startham Hall a signpost points the way, away from the track, along the left edge of the grounds of the house. Go over the stile into a small fenced field. Walk half right towards a stile on the other side of the field. Now go straight along a well worn path through the middle of a field. This arrives at a lane. Follow it to the right. It soon bends to the left, becoming a hedged lane. There is a small pond to the left. At a T-junction of paths, turn left and then soon to the right. This path carries you through the fields. After passing wooden fencing on the left, the path swings to the right and then to the left again. It continues uphill. At a track to the right the longer and shorter routes divide.

2. *Longer Route:*

With the hedge to the left and a field to the right, continue uphill until arriving at the spoil tip. Turn right down the path, noticing the stone surface. This is Garswood Road, the old miners road. Pass through the copse. Ignore the path to the right immediately after it, but as you continue along the wide

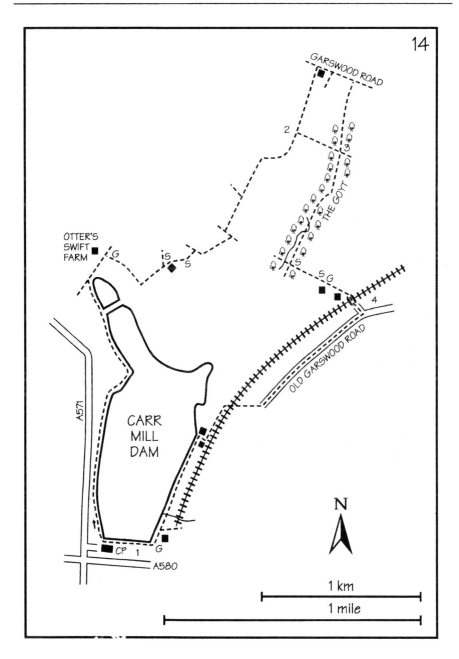

fern strewn way, soon look for another path on the right. This takes you along the right edge of the gully and trees. The path goes, at a pond to the right, into the slightly wider woodland of the Goyt. At a wide farm track, meet the shorter route at point 3.

Shorter Route:

Turn right along the wide track. This has small trees along its right edge. Pass through a dip and carry on until reaching a narrow strip of woodland on both sides of the track. A well-worn path will be seen coming in from the left and continuing into the trees on the right. This is the meeting point with the longer route.

3. Follow the path into the woodland. This is a longish section. After a while, having passed through an open fern area and by a pond on the right, cross a stream coming in from the left. The path now continues to the left of the stream. Soon after the path crosses the stream again and then quickly back over it and up the steepish bank on the other side. At a split of paths for a few metres a little later, take the one to the right to avoid the branches of a fallen tree. Follow the left bank of the stream, until reaching a crossroad of paths.

A stile and footbridge will be seen over to the right, but instead take either the steep path to the left or the more gentle one a few metres further on. Almost immediately, at the top of the short slope, go over a big stile. Keep to the fence, interspersed with bushes, on the left of the field, continue by the stile and gate up the wide farm track, with a fence on both sides. Over the gate at the end of it, go by the large house and then the buildings of Hollin Hey Farm. After the entrance to the farm and going through a gate, go by the farm house and over the high sided railway bridge. From the bridge, go the few metres to the T-junction with another section of Garswood Road.

4. Here turn right. The road is a narrow metal country lane, bordered by woods and fields. After a while, St Helens can be seen to the left, across the fields. Pass a wide track entering the woods on the right. The metal road soon after swings to the left through a gate and continues across a field. Just before the gate, a wide dirt track goes ahead and passes beneath the railway embankment. Turn left and follow the path, which runs parallel to the embankment. With a path going into the woods on the right, continue ahead at the two white topped posts. At the end of the path, it swings to the right through two sets of barriers and emerges, with a white building ahead.

Turn left and almost immediately left in front of the power boat club. Follow the very wide track along. The lake, on the right, is hidden from view by fences and then a wall. A break in the wall enables a good view across the lake to be seen. On the left is the railway viaduct. Underneath it runs the Black Brook, which flows on into the Sankey Valley.

Keep straight on along the wide track, which now has a better surface. Ignoring a path to the left which leads back down to the brook, pass a cottage on the left and go through a gate, to reach the point at which the walk started.

15. Earlestown

This walk takes in open fields and a section of the
St Helens Canal.

Route: Earlestown – Bradlegh Old Hall – Burtonwood – Canal –
               Earlestown.

Start: Redbrow Car Park. Grid reference 577 944.

Distance: 5 or $4\frac{1}{2}$ miles.

Duration: 2 or $1\frac{3}{4}$ hours.

Map: SJ 49/59

By train: Earlestown station. To reach the start is a walk of half a mile. From
               the station go left up Queen Street. Soon after, turn left into Earle
               Street. Then turn left, over the rail bridge, into Junction Lane. Follow
               the road through the industrial estate. A few hundred metres after
               passing the recycling centre, which is on your right, turn left down
               the wide metal road, with white centre markings. Walking on the
               pathway to the left of the road, follow it as it swings to the right. By
               a factory on the left, the pathway goes downhill to the left, as the
               road bends sharply to the right. Keep on the pathway until Redbrow
               car park is reached.

By car: From the A580 (East Lancashire Road) take the A49 into
               Newton-le-Willows. Turn right at the first roundabout onto the A572
               road to St Helens. After the traffic lights, turn left into Victoria Road
               just after the pedestrian lights and the Catholic Church. Go under
               the railway bridge. Continue until reaching the Victoria pub on the
               right. The signs point down Bradlegh Road to Newton Community
               Hospital and Sankey Valley car park. Go over the bridge. As the
               road swings sharply to the left, continue straight ahead down the
               dirt track to the car park by the canal.

Refreshments: Earlestown centre and Fiddle i'th Bag pub.

1. From the car park cross the swing bridge over the canal and then the red bridge over the brook. Go to the right along the path, which gradually goes uphill through the trees, moving away from the valley. Reaching the T-junction of paths at the top of the rise, the way is along the wide path to the left. However, it is worth going a few metres along the path to the right to gain a view towards the Sankey viaduct. The first passenger railway train in the world passed over it in 1830. A little more railway history will be seen later in the walk.

Go back along the path and continue straight ahead. The wide dirt track makes its way through open fields, with a line of pylons passing through them. Immediately beyond a gate, a farm track passes across the path. To the right is Bradlegh Old Hall Farm, which was formerly a fortified manor house. To the left can be seen New Bradley Hall Farm.

Coming to the road, turn right into Hall Lane. Pass, on the right, a gas marker (No 20) surrounded by a little forest of white stones. At the next road junction, look for the sign-posted footpath on the other side of the road, just to the left of the house named Ingleholme. On the left of the road is a 40 mph sign by Boarded Barn Farm. For most of the length of the path, there is a wooden fence on the left, beyond which are houses. To the right are fields, with a row of telegraph poles going across. A lonely cottage is also to be seen.

After passing the end of a cul-de-sac, which is on the left, the path becomes a metal one. There is waste ground to the right. Cross a small road. Now there is a stream to the left. Go over the footbridge. There is now a row of trees on the left. After wooden fence on the left and hedge on the right, arrive at another busier road. This is now the village of Burtonwood. It was well known during the second world war for the nearby United States forces base.

2. Cross the road and go along what is at first a wide path. By a small garage to the left, the path narrows. It continues, with houses on both sides, after the cemetery to the right.

After crossing a stream, the path emerges into fields. Do not take the path to the left, but go ahead on, keeping to the right of the hedge. As the hedge ends, the path goes on, with a ditch to the left and a barbed wire fence on the right. As the path rises higher from the ditch, the smoking chimneys of Fiddlers Ferry power station can be seen in the distance. After a short distance of cart track, come to a well-signposted junction of paths.

Turn left and go along the wide farm track, with trees and hedges on either side. This leads to a gate, with a stile on its left. Over the stile, you are in the Burtonwood Nature Reserve. There are picnic tables available, if you have brought a packed lunch. Keep to the path that goes ahead, along the hedge side. Go over a footbridge, and turn right along a path, which comes in from the left. There are houses to the left and bowling greens to the right. Reach the sign at the road, which indicates Green Jones Brow. Turn right, over the stream, along the road.

3. There is a choice of routes here:

Long Route:

Turn right into Farmers Lane. As the road turns sharply right at Tan House Farm, go straight ahead along the unsigned track. At the three-way signpost, turn left along the left-hand side of the ditch and small shrubs. As the ditch starts to bear to the right, look for the waymarker which points at an angle to the left across the field towards a lone tallish tree by a pond. On reaching the pond, turn right at the next waymarker along the right side of a ditch. As this ends, continue ahead, passing an old redundant gate post. Go straight on through the next field, keeping the rows of short wooden posts to the left. Arrive at the road to meet the shorter route at point 4.

Shorter Route:

Pass Farmers Lane and continue up the road for a short distance. After a small field on the right, come to a playing field. Just before the bus stop, turn right along the edge of the

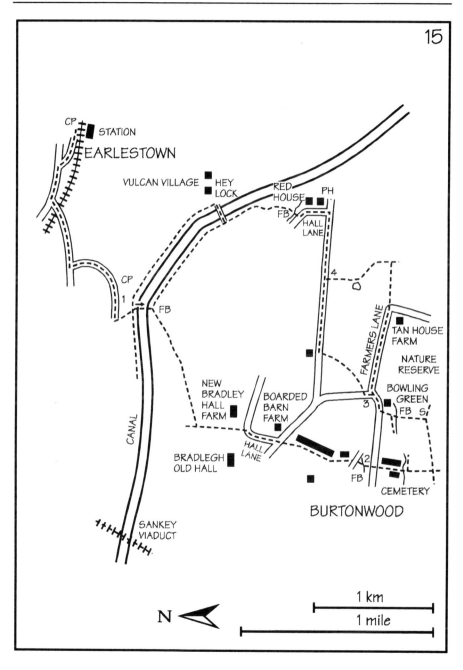

15

CP
STATION
EARLESTOWN
VULCAN VILLAGE · HEY
· LOCK
RED
HOUSE
PH
FB
HALL
LANE
CP
4
D
1
FB
FARMERS LANE
TAN HOUSE
FARM
NATURE
RESERVE
NEW
BRADLEY
HALL
FARM
BOARDED
BARN
FARM
BOWLING
GREEN
FB S
CANAL
3
HALL
LANE
BRADLEGH
OLD HALL
2
FB
CEMETERY
BURTONWOOD
SANKEY
VIADUCT

1 km

1 mile

N

playing field, with a hedge to the right. Reach the road, opposite to a house. Turn right and walk along the pavement.

4. From the meeting point of the longer and shorter routes continué, passing Cooper's Farm shop. (If a break is needed, immediately past the left turn into Hall Lane is the Fiddle I'th Bag pub.) Go left along Hall Lane. Just after Red Delph Farm, a signpost points to the right. Follow the short path to the bridge over the brook. Then go on the path ahead through the fields. Always bending to the right, it arrives at the canal towpath, by a seat. Across the canal can be seen the factory of Rushton Diesels. This was the original site of the Vulcan Foundry of 1830. This was associated with Robert Stephenson, the son of Charles, who built the Liverpool to Manchester first passenger railway.

Walk left along the towpath, soon arriving at Hey Lock. This was originally known as Vulcan Lock, because of the foundry mentioned above. Here is a choice of ways. Either stay on the path, which is the easier flatter walk back to the finish of the

Canal path at Earlestown

walk, or cross to the other side of the canal, turn left and follow the path through the woods. The path is narrower and more up and down than the towpath route. The towpath arrives back at the first bridge crossed at the start of the walk. Cross it back to the car-park. The woodland path arrives directly back at the car-park.

16. Bold

*Known in past years for its coal mines, the area around Bold is
now peaceful countryside, the previous spoil heaps now
reclaimed and landscaped.*

Route: Clock Face – Bold Hall – Bold Heath – Clock Face.

Start: Gorsey Lane, Clock Face. Grid reference: 519 912.

Distance: 6 miles.

Duration: 2½ hours.

Maps: SJ 48/58 and SJ 49/59.

By car: Clock Face is situated on the A570, half a mile north of the M62 (no
                  direct access from the motorway). Travelling north, Gorsey Lane is
                  the first main turning right on reaching the built up area. It is easy
                  to park by turning first right from Gorsey Lane into Bushel's Lane.

Refreshments: Griffin Inn and Maplewood Restaurant at Bold Heath halfway round
                  the walk.

---

1. Walk to the right along Gorsey Lane, keeping the pavement
on the right. After the end of the housing, there are fields to
the left and a fence along reclaimed colliery land to the right.
On reaching large ex-mine buildings on the left, part of which
are now occupied by small firms, cross the road. At the far
end of the buildings is a footpath sign from the road. Turn left
along the path. At the beginning there are trees on both sides.
Walk beside the perimeter fence of the buildings. The path
continues through the fields, with a ditch to the right. In the
dip, just beyond the line of poles, turn right at the crossroad
of paths.

Along this path, there is a ditch to the right, with occasional
small trees. This is a longish stretch of pathway. Along it the
poles swap from side to side of the route. Pass a pond,
surrounded by trees, which is on the left. The ditch ends
shortly before reaching another crossroad of paths. Keep

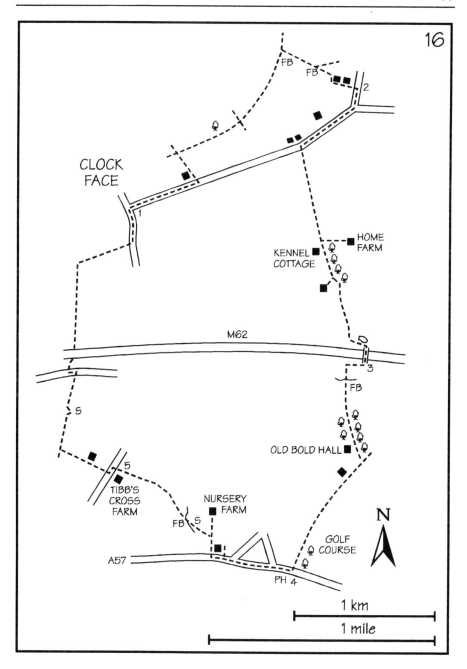

straight on over the cart track. Soon the ditch on the right resumes again. After passing a line of trees by the ditch, the poles start to swing away to the left. Soon after crossing a wooden reinforcement on the path, you come to a bridge without rails, immediately by a bush.

Go right across the bridge and through the fields, which are crossed by large pylons. Next there is a ditch and barbed wire fencing on the right. Now look for a footbridge across the ditch. Do not take the main track which goes on, swinging away to the left.

Cross the footbridge and go left. There are railings of the horse paddock to the right and a pond on the left. Turn right at the garden walls and soon left into the wide roadway of Rosemary Lane, with houses to the left. At the road, with a phone kiosk on the corner, turn right into Neill's Road.

2. Then turn right into another section of Gorsey Lane. There is woodland to the left. Pass the Northfield Riding Centre, which is on the right. On arriving at a wood on the left, turn left,

Kennel Cottage

opposite two houses, along Hall Lane. This is indicated by a footpath sign, which also prohibits horse-riding.

Then pass a home made sign, which tries to deter vehicles.

Along the lane there is a stone wall on the left protecting the woodland. To the right, across the fields, can be seen a large reclaimed spoil heap. After passing the entrance to Home Farm and the lovely Kennel Cottage, the lane gets a little stonier. As it ends at a house to the right, go left by a gate on the left, still staying at the edge of the woodland.

You are now on the cart track. At the end of the wood, follow the track bearing to the right, across the middle of the fields. The M62 can now be seen in the distance. The track makes for the end of the line of trees on the left edge of the field. Reaching here, turn left by the side of the pond and go the short distance to the bridge over the motorway.

3. On the other side, follow the waymark round to the stile to the right. Over the stile, walk along parallel to the motorway. Go left at the footpath sign and waymark. Cross over the wooden bridge that spans the stream. Follow the track that heads through the fields towards the woods. At the entrance to the woods is a sign. For some reason this and the next two signs point only in the opposite direction to that of our walk. After wending its way through the woodland, the path shortly comes to the buildings of Old Bold Hall Farm. The Bold family lived at the Manor House for many centuries. As you come to another footpath sign, go through the old gate post and bridge across the moat. This was all part of the rebuilt Hall of 1616.

Continue ahead to the next more modern sign post. Now turn right down the wide lane, with the farm buildings on the right.

The lane is quite a long one. The hedge to the right becomes a low one. The telegraph wire eventually go right, alongside a lane to a farm on the right. By a copse and stream on the left are the grounds of the Mersey Valley Golf Club. Go over another stream to arrive at Warrington Road, opposite to the Bold Heath Equestrian Centre.

4. Turn right, passing Clock Face Road and School Lane, as well as the Griffin Inn and Maplewood Restaurant. Immediately after School Lane, do not take the path that leads into the wood, but continue along. Just after Holly House, turn right up the drive of Nursery Farm. If the gate is closed, go over the stile and along the tree-shaped avenue. The farm is now a private house. Just before reaching it, turn left along the garden path. There is a ditch and a line of trees to the left. Then, after a very short grass section, as the garden path goes to the right, arrive at a stile.

Follow the footpath sign along the left edge of the field. As the ditch bends to the right, cross over the footbridge. Then proceed along the right edge of the next field, with the ditch on the right. After a while, a footpath sign points across the field towards a hawthorn hedge. Walk to the right of this to reach the farm road.

5. Turn left and, immediately opposite to Tibb's Cross Farm, turn up the wide path towards a house. Keep to the left of the house and go ahead, with the hedge on your right. At the fence of the old St Helens and Runcorn Gap railway, turn right at the signpost and go along the edge of the field. As the ground slopes down to a stream, go up a short slope to the left and over the stile. Continue along the left edge of the field, parallel to the old railway. On reaching the road, by a signpost, turn left over the bridge at Union Bank Lane. Then turn right immediately along a railed path. Follow it as it goes under the M62, but above the old railway. On the other side, continue on the path. The fencing of the old spoil heap is to the left and the railway down below.

As the path drops to the level of the old railway, look for a long fence on the far side of it. Cross the track bed and follow the railing, walking to the right of them. At the end of the railings there are houses to the right. At the road, turn left and then right into Gorsey Lane.

17. Warrington

A haunted hall and an old graving dock are features of this walk around the lower Sankey Valley.

Route: Waterways – Bewsey Old Hall – Causey Bridge – Gemini – Waterways.

Start: Sankey Valley car park. Grid reference: 588 887.

Distance: 5½ miles.

Duration: 2¾ hours.

Maps: SJ 48/58 and SJ 49/59.

By car: From the roundabout where the A57 and A562 join, there are traffic lights ¼ miles due east. From these, drive north the short distance along Cromwell Avenue to a mini-roundabout. Turn right, following the Sankey Valley Park sign, a few hundred metres along a narrow road to the car park.

Refreshments: The Hoop and Mallet and Bewsey Farm Inn.

---

1. From the car park, access the canal adjacent to the valley map. Go left along the canal bank, passing the bridge. Then there is woodland on the left. Ignore the path coming in from the left and continue to the seven viaducts railway bridge. With paths coming in from the left along the way, keep to the canal bank. There is a slight bend in the path as it goes past a pond and then swampy land.

Just as you reach the bridge, pass through the gate as the path bears left. It is worth following the second path to the left, which is marked Bewsey Old Hall Ranger Centre. Go along the stone path, with a hedge to the left and soon turn right at the railings. Follow the track as it bears left to the Old Hall. The main part of the hall is now unused and boarded up, but there is a small information room which is normally open.

The hall was the seat of the Boteler family, who were Lords of Warrington from the twelfth century. The first building was

Bewsey Old Hall

erected in 1264, but the present one dates from the sixteenth century. Both Henry VII and James I stayed at the hall. Sir John Boteler, the 12th Lord was murdered here in the fifteenth century. It is said that his wife Isobella, the White Lady of Bewsey, haunts the hall and grounds.

From the hall, retrace your steps to the white timbered house by the canal bridge. Cross the railed bridge and then drop back down to the path on the left on the other side. Do not take the path that goes higher up round the electricity sub-station. Soon after passing through the gateway, with the rails to the left and trees to the right, do not cross the bridge over the canal but continue on.

You are now on a wide farm track. The canal on the left is a disused section. The ground on the right is higher than the track. Houses will be seen ahead. As the track reaches the Sankey Brook coming in from the right, it becomes more narrow and swings to the left to the other side of the disused canal bed. By the bushes, turn right along the grass track by the brook. Do not go onto the tarmac track nearby.

Make for the left side of the footbridge ahead. Go through the

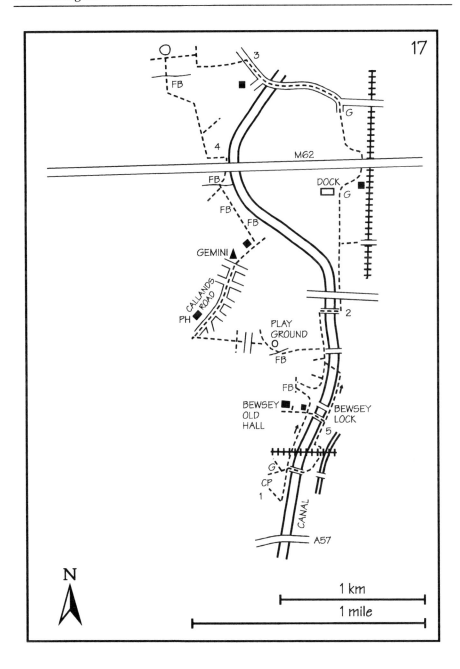

narrow opening in the railings on both sides of the pathway that crosses the bridge. Continue on along the grass track on the left-hand side of the brook. After more houses on the far side of the brook, the tower of Winwick Church will be seen ahead in the far distance. Much nearer is a road bridge and, a few hundred metres in front of it, a footbridge.

Over the footbridge, turn left, ignoring the other paths. Proceed under the road bridge. Pass two stone pillars, which act as car barriers. Do not take the path to the right, but go onto the grass track by the brook. Ignore all the right turns into the landscaped park-land. The path becomes a dirt track, with now open ground to the left. After a path coming in from the railway footbridge on the right, pass the railings around the old dock. This reminds you that you are walking on the filled in old canal. The M6 can be seen and heard ahead and there are factories to the right. Pass a path with horseshoe bridle path sign to the right and then another path. Then there is a low bank on the left.

After the old dry dock of Winwick Quay on the left, go through the gate with the horse entrance beside it. This leads to a path, with rails on the right-hand side, which gradually bend to the right. The buildings to the right, one of which has 1841 on it, were the old canal repair buildings. Take the tarmac path as it goes left under the motorway, parallel to the railway. Try to ignore the unsightly car repair centre ahead. The road swings left by it and then right by a gate, which threatens a £4,000 fine for tipping.

The metal road then goes on, with open fields looking towards the M6 and the Fiddlers Ferry power station. It runs parallel to the railway and the filled in canal to the right. One of the canal locks can still be seen along the way. Eventually you come to a car barrier, with a gate at the side, across the road. Through it, you are on Alder Lane. Turn left and follow the unfenced road as it bends left. There are woods to be seen ahead and pylons crossing the field to the right. You are walking parallel to the M6. Pass the Winwick sign and cross Causey Bridge.

A second bridge, with a TV aerial on a very small shed, takes you over the Sankey Brook. To the left is Causeway Bridges Farm. The notice on the lane to it indicates Private Road. This is, in fact, not true, because it is a public right of way. However, the footpath sign, which you will pass later at the other end of the lane has the indicator broken off. Assuming that the farm owner does not like walkers, we will leave this path to inveterate ramblers, and walk a little further up the road.

An old footpath sign, looking a little the worse for wear, will be seen on the right-hand side of the road. It points to the left, along the right-hand side of the hedge. The pylons run parallel to it. After a gap in it, the hedge bends gradually to the right, while the pylons carry straight on. Pass a post with a way-marker on it and a clump of trees. After another way marker, a stream on the left goes off at a sharp angle, just before two dead trees. After passing under wires, come to a lone tree. Turn 90° to the right and make for a three way footpath sign. At it, turn left onto the farm track. After a few hundred metres, with small trees surrounding a pond on the right, turn left along another farm track. This makes its way through the middle of the large field and over the stream by means of a flat stone bridge.

On reaching another three way footpath sign, turn left towards a lone tree a distance away, with Winwick spire in the distance behind it. After passing the tree, you reach yet another three-way sign. (This is the one with the broken pointer referred to earlier). Go ahead towards the motorway, keeping to the right of the hedge.

At the motorway follow the sign to the left. You will see a larger one indicating 'Gullivers World', but this is of more interest to motorway drivers. At the end of the motorway fence, follow the sign to the right, along the wide concrete path under the motorway. Emerging, follow a wide track as it bends to the right. Cross over the stream by means of the footbridge to the left, ignoring the path ahead. At the small triangle of grass, take the path ahead. This brings you on to a long section of landscaped pathway, which runs along the back of the industrial estate, after going down the steps and across the footbridge, opposite to Fyffes' factory. Another footbridge is crossed, before the path comes to an end at a T-junction. Here turn right. The path takes you by the car park of Europa House, into a small park and out onto the road by the tall construction, somewhat like a rocket, which is the logo of the Gemini industrial estate. There is now a few minutes of road work to contend with. Go straight on to the roundabout ahead. Cross the busy Cromwell Avenue into Callands Road. Pass St David's Road and Gresford Close on the left. Soon after the Hoop and Mallet Inn on the right , turn left down a tarmac path, with stone bollards across it. Go down the path, passing an entrance coming in on the left from Gresford Close. At a cross road of paths keep straight on. After crossing a road, the path continues through an avenue of trees. After this, turn right towards the children's playground. Follow the path through the playground and straight on, ignoring all paths coming in from the right.

After a pond on the right, cross the footbridge over the stream and immediately turn left at the T-junction. Arriving at a cross road of paths (the one to the left leading across a bridge), take the one straight ahead. To the left, you will notice the bed of the disused canal, the opposite side of which was used on the outward journey. A small stream along the line of bushes is the only remnant of the water filled basin.

Follow the wide track along the edge of the basin, with open ground to the right. Do not cross the next footbridge, but take the one to the right going into the woods. After winding its way through the trees, it comes to a T-junction. Turn left over the footbridge. Follow the path to the left by the water and then to the right as it goes towards Bewsey Old Hall. Arrive back at the black and white house.

Turn left across the bridge used earlier in the walk, then right along the canal bank. After passing a picnic table, the trees come closer to the canal bank. At the railway bridge, there is a notice indicating the Wetland Nature Reserve. Go straight ahead under the bridge and then immediately left away from the canal. Turn right and follow the bank of the Sankey Brook until reaching a double bridge. Just before the bridges, the Wetlands viewing platform is to the right.

Take the bridge to the right, across the canal. Go ahead, through a gate, back to the car park.

18. Cronton

Pex Hill with its quarry dominates the surrounding countryside. The walk is flat, with only one short incline towards the end.

Route: Pex Hill – Upton – Cronton Hall – Pex Hill.

Start: Pex Hill Visitor Centre. Grid reference: 502 888

Distance: 4½ miles.

Duration: 2½ hours.

Map: SJ 48/58

By car: Turn off the A5080 opposite Widnes Sixth Form College. Grid reference: 504 883. Follow the road, through the green railings, to the Visitors Centre at the top of the hill.

Refreshments: The Unicorn Inn in Cronton and the Tavern in Upton.

---

1. From the Visitors Centre, take the path towards the far end of the fence of the quarry. At the end of the path, with the notice pointing to the centre back behind you, take the track to the left. This has low wooden railings on both sides as it passes through the trees.

Go by a gate and, with a house on the right, turn right down the lane that you have previously driven up to the Centre. At the bottom of the lane, opposite to the Sixth Form College, go right past the Cronton road sign. Walk on the far pavement. After passing Cronton Nurseries, turn left off the road, at a signpost opposite to a house.

The path takes you through the fields to a wooded glade. The path now continues on the right-hand side of a field. Then it becomes a cart track, bearing left across the field towards a lone tree. Runcorn Bridge can be seen in the distance over to the right. The path goes on to reach the road by some houses on the left-hand side. Turn left along the road. If there is need for refreshments at this stage, then carry on for a few hundred metres to the Tavern Inn. If not, turn right almost

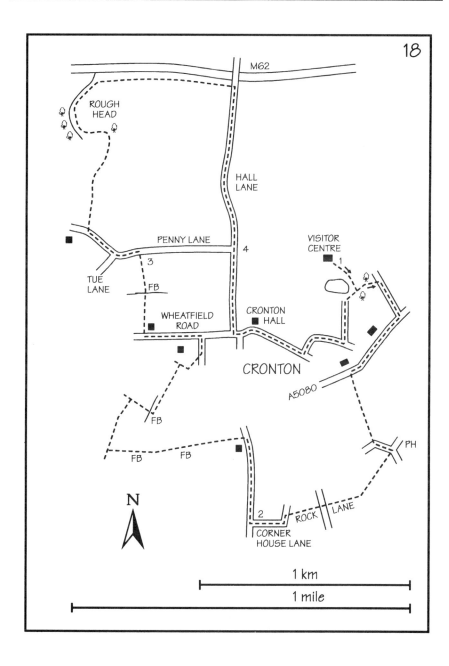

immediately. To the right is a sign indicating 'Bridlepath. Access to Rock Lane only'.

The wide track goes diagonally across the field. When it reaches a dip at the other side, do not follow the wide track which continues along the field but go down the dip and turn right onto Rock Lane. The lane is a pathway between an avenue of trees. On reaching a road, cross over to the gap in the wooden railings. Then follow the lane, with a ditch on the left, the short distance to another road. Turn left along the road bending to the right through a housing estate.

2. At the T-junction, with the name plate Cornerhouse Lane displayed on the left corner, turn right. Eventually pass a signpost to the right. Then, after two houses on a bend, turn left at the footpath sign, which directs you down some steps, through two stone pillars, into the field. Aim straight ahead for a short pole, with a waymarker on it. The land to the right is now somewhat higher. Continue ahead, with a ditch on the right. Cross a footbridge and later a second one. At the second, there is a hedge going away towards the houses on the left. Continue on the short distance to a footpath sign in the middle of the field. Here turn right. Follow the track until it reaches a waymarked post at a junction of paths.

Follow the waymarker to the right. After crossing over a boardbridge, follow left along the edge of the ditch. A farm is nearby. As the track to the farm goes to the left, go to the right, with a ditch on both sides. The path then comes to a dirt lane. Turn left and go the short distance to the road. Cross the road to the footpath on the other side. Pass Wheatfield Road. After the last building on the right, a bungalow, take the footpath to the right at the signpost.

The path goes through the fields towards the trees. Then there is a ditch, with a hedge along it, on the right. Cross a two railed footbridge over Fox's Bank Brook. Pylons cross the fields ahead. Over to the left is a copse, with an aerial in the centre. Carry on across the fields until reaching Penny Lane at a footpath sign.

3. There is a choice here:

Shorter Walk:

Turn right along Penny Lane. Join the route of the longer walk at the junction of Penny Lane with Hall Lane.

Longer Walk:

Turn left, but do not proceed along Tue Lane. Rather bear right along the continuation of Penny Lane. Just before the farm, turn right at the signpost, onto a farm track. This heads towards the M62 in the distance. There is a ditch to the left. After a while the track becomes more grassy and there is a ditch on both sides, with a line of trees on the right.

The path sinks a little lower than the land to the left. At a lone tree, a waymarker directs along the path to the left in the direction of Rough Head Wood. The path then goes along the right-hand edge of the wood. There is a pond on the left and soon a stream. Follow the stream round to the right along the edge of the field, heading directly for the motorway. At the

Cronton Hall

M62 the stream disappears into a culvert. Turn right along the edge of the motorway. The track then gradually moves away from it to reach the Hall Lane Bridge. Go up the steps, with a signpost at the top, onto the road.

Turn right along Hall Lane. There is no pavement along this section of the walk, so be particularly careful. Eventually pass Penny Lane, which is on the right. This is where the shorter walk joints the longer one.

4. With Smithy Lane going off to the right, follow Hall Lane around to the left. Pass Cronton Hall, which has a footpath sign by it directing to Rainhill. Later turn left up to the Roundabout. Follow the road round to the right. At a sharp right-hand bend in the road, there is a wide track going off to the left. Go along this, gradually ascending, until reaching the quarry at the top. Turn right along the quarry railings and then left back to the Visitors Centre.

19. Halewood

The track o the old Cheshire Lines Railway links country footpaths on the edge of Halewood Village.

Route: Halewood Village – Loop Line – Foxhill House – Halewood Village.

Start: Okell Drive Visitor Centre, Halewood. Grid reference: 440 863.

Distance: 4 miles.

Duration: 2 hours.

Map: SJ 48/58

Train: Halewood Station is on Merseyrail. From the station pick the walk up at Stage No.3.

By car: From the junction of the M62 and M57 take the road signposted to Huyton. At the traffic lights turn left in to Whitefield Lane, then left again into Netherley Road. Next, first right into Green's Bridge Lane. Having reached the public house, turn right into Church Road. Having passed the Eagle and Child and the Parish Church, at the roundabout turn left into Okell Drive. After a right bend, reach the Visitor Centre.

Refreshments: Eagle and Child, Church Road.

---

1. The Visitor Centre is at Halewood Country Park, which is run by the Knowsley Ranger Service. It is on the site of the old Cheshire Lines Railway, which became disused in 1964. The pathway in all extends 10 miles from Halewood to Aintree. It is hoped that the missing link through Aintree will be soon found to link the Loop Line with the Cheshire Lines path from Maghull to Southport.

From the Centre car-park, take the track going northwards, indicated by the footpath sign to Gateacre. The route travels through the trees of one of the few remaining tracts of wood in the Merseyside region. At a junction of paths, with a four-way sign, carry ahead over the bridge across the stream. Some new houses can be seen to the right.

There is a bridle-path to the right of the main track. Open fields can be glimpsed to the left and railings in the tree to the right. Cross the bridge over Lydiate Lane. The track begins gradually to rise. There are extensive views away over to the right. Go on through a bridge with unsightly breezeblock sides. After a path coming in from the left and crossing the next old railway bridge, look for some steep steps with black railing, going down the embankment to the right.

2. At the foot of the steps, a tunnel can be seen going back under the embankment. There is a short length of wire fence on the right. Follow the path through the nature reserve, going right at the fork. There are railings to the right. At the junction of paths turn right and then left, following the footpath sign to Gerrards Lane.

For the next quarter of a mile, the path goes between the fence of the water-treatment plant. Gerrards Brook is on the left, with a large pipe running just above it. At a clump of trees, pass over a side stream. Continue ahead, as the path passes beneath the large pipe. The building of the water-treatment plant can be seen to the right. On the left is the Lee Park Golf Course. At a footpath sign, the stream goes away to the left. Follow the fence along the edge of the field towards the trees, keeping the hedge to your left. Through the trees, turn right along the lane. This widens, with houses on either side. At Church Road, turn left by the Eagle and Child and immediately right into Hollies Road. Pass the Community Centre and 9th Knowsley Scouts Headquarters. Cross Crantock Close.

3. Just after Plantation Primary School and before Halewood Station, turn right at the large signpost pointing to Gateacre and Okell Drive. The path goes for a while along the edge of the school field and then bears left up onto the embankment. Walk on through the trees along the wide path. Pass a seat and a cross path. Then go by a gate and across Rainbow Drive to continue on the path.

Soon you will see the Triangle sculpture. Go under this and then you are back at the Visitors Centre and car-park.

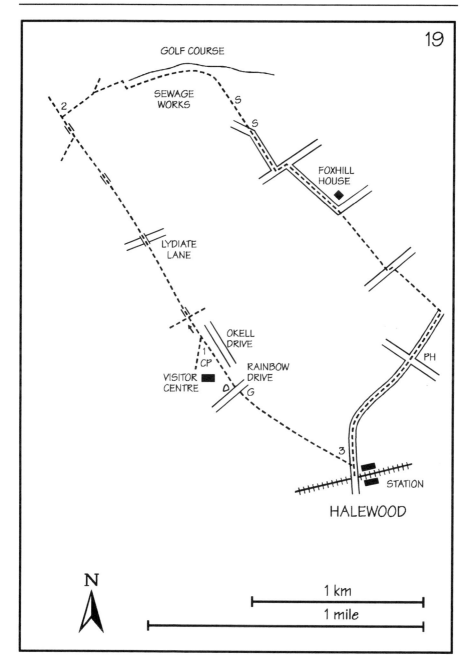

The Halewood Triangle

20. Hale

Hale Village is one of the hidden gems of Merseyside. This easy walk takes in the lovely thatched cottages of the village and the banks of the Mersey Estuary.

Route: Hale Village – Hale Head Lighthouse – Within Way – Hale Village.

Start: Hale Village Centre. Grid reference: 469 833.

Distance: 5 or 4 miles.

Duration: 2½ or 2 miles.

Map: SJ 48/58.

By car: Hale is immediately east of Liverpool Airport and Speke. Parking is in the park opposite to the Post Office and Stores.

Refreshments: Childe of Hale, Hale Village Centre.

---

1. Turn left from the park, passing the Hale Carriage Company on the left. The cottages on both sides of the road are old. Continue along, with Cocklade Lane and Aran Close over on the right. On reaching Remsbrook Lane, which goes away to the right, bear left into Hale Road. After Hale Garage on the left, there is a row of poplar trees on the right.

Soon after passing the service station, turn left into Baileys Lane. For a short distance there are houses on both sides of the road, then open fields with the occasional house. In the fields to the right are warning lights for the nearby Speke airport. Towards the end of the lane are yellow lines on the road and a sign stating 'stop when the lights flash'. Turn left, with the airfield railings on the right.

At a sign indicating 'Mersey Way – Garston Foreshore' do not follow the road round to the right in the direction indicated, but carry straight on, over a crossroad of paths and through a kissing gate. The wide path slopes down towards the river. When the copse of trees comes to an end, turn left on the path sloping upwards. This brings you up onto Hale Cliff, high above the foreshore.

2. Proceed along the path, passing a short length of old wire fencing and a seat. There are fields to the left, with houses in the distance. Arriving at a copse, go down the wooden steps, over the railed footbridge and follow the steps up the other side. With a large house, immediately to he left, continue along the cliff path, with fields to the left and a wood in the distance. There are the posts of long defunct fences dotted along the way. Ignore a path that goes left into the wood.

After a lone tree on the left, there are trees between the path and the cliff edge, plus a length of barbed wire fence on the left. With trees on both sides of the path, go past a path into the woods on the left and immediately arrive at a footpath sign, by a seat and steps down to the short.

Carry straight on. There is now a long length of barbed wire fencing in good repair on the left. You are heading towards the lighthouse in the distance. After going over a footbridge, there is now no fence on the left. After passing a seat, the lighthouse is reached at Hale Head. It is no longer functional and is a private house nowadays. Here the Mersey estuary is at its widest. In the distance can be seen the Stanlow Oil Refinery and Ellesmere Port.

3. There is a choice:

Shorter Walk:

From the lighthouse, go left, away from the river, up Lighthouse Road. At the end of this path, go on to the metalled road and continue until reaching St Mary's Church. Here meet the route of the longer walk.

Longer Walk:

From the lighthouse, follow the footpath sign. The path goes along the side of the lighthouse garden and passes two seats along the way. There are small bushes to the right and rising land to the left. The path is level with the shoreline. Runcorn

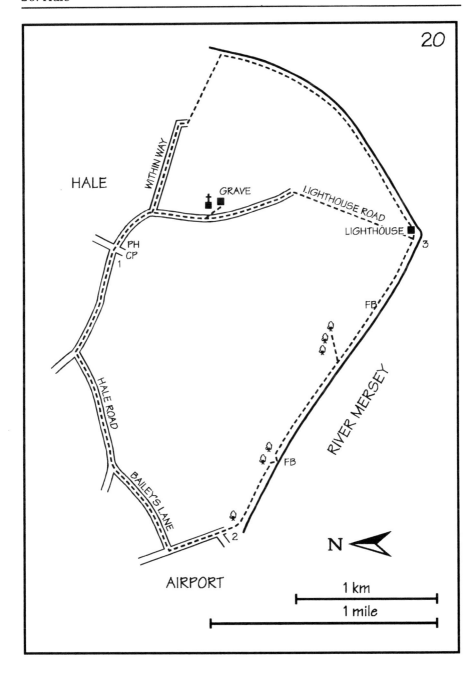

20

HALE

WITHIN WAY

GRAVE

LIGHTHOUSE ROAD

LIGHTHOUSE

3

PH
CP
1

HALE ROAD

BAILEY'S LANE

FB

RIVER MERSEY

FB

2

AIRPORT

N

1 km

1 mile

Wood sculpture opposite church

Bridge can be seen in the distance. A footpath sign is reached, as the path comes onto a wider lane. This is Within Way. At the point, travellers of old used to ford the river. Sometimes this included herds of cattle and sheep. Even with intimate local knowledge of the tides, this was a hazardous undertaking. Many a life was lost during attempted crossings. The word Within means willow, the name coming from the willow groves in the vicinity.

Take the track as it makes inland, with a fence to the left and a ditch to the right. Coming to a gate and footpath sign, continue along what is now a wider road. This bends to the right and then swings back to the left. The road becomes metal as it goes on. After a farm on the left, turn left into Church Lane. After a few metres come to the Church of St Mary, restored after a disastrous fire of some years ago. Through the lych-gate and on the far side of the building is to be found the grave of the Childe of Hale. This giant of nine feet six inches lived from 1578-1623 and once wrestled at the court of James I. On the opposite side of the road from the Church the remains of a dead tree has been carved into a resemblance of a totem pole.

From the Church, retrace your footsteps, passing by Within Way again. Notice the row of thatched cottages on the left. Just beyond the Childe of Hale pub, you will find yourself back at the village centre and at the end of the journey.

Also of interest:

WEST LANCASHIRE WALKS

This is the companion to EAST LANCASHIRE WALKS, also written by the 'rambling clergyman' Michael Smout. They are perfect for people in search of shorter walks. None is longer than six miles, but they are all packed with information and are ideal for family groups. *£6.95*

50 CLASSIC WALKS IN LANCASHIRE

Terry Marsh

Enjoy Lancashire at its best with these fifty glorious walks. There are short woodland walks, riverside rambles and invigorating excursions on the West Pennine Moors and in the Forest of Bowland – truly a walk for every occasion and every mood. There is a bonus to each walks - an insight into local history, an example of industrial archaeology, illustrations of geological formation or views of spectacular scenery. There's a spellbinding excursion into Pendle witch country, a glimpse of the past at Hornby Castle and a bracing walk in the wilderness of the Forest of Bowland.

£7.95

Tea Shop Walks to Savour!

TEA SHOP WALKS IN LANCASHIRE

Clive Price

Clive Price's selection of 30 walks through Lancashire – taking in the best tea-rooms on the way – is a must for all locals and visitors to the county. From flagged floors to luxurious carpets, from a medieval barn to a working Post Office, the tea shops really are something special – and you can be sure the food is as good as the setting! The routes vary in length from 4 to 10 miles, so are suitable for all the family. They encompass lush riverside pastures and high, open moorlands and one enjoys the centre of Lancaster itself, with its ancient castle and Priory Church. As you explore both town and country, you can be sure of the reward of a delicious afternoon tea on the way!

In the same series:

Tea Shop Walks in the Chilterns

Tea Shop Walks in Surrey & Sussex

Tea Shop Walks in Shropshire

Tea Shop Walks in South Devon

Tea Shop Walks in the Cotswolds

Tea Shop Walks in the Lake District

Tea Shop Walks in the Peak District

Tea Shop Walks in the Yorkshire Dales

All temptingly priced at £6.95!

BEST PUB WALKS IN LANCASHIRE

Neil Coates

Lancashire has a rich pub heritage, many excellent local breweries and a surprising variety of countryside for invigorating walks, all liable to build up a thirst! To solve the problem of where to combine the finest walks with the most notable hostelries, Neil Coates has written the most comprehensive guidebook of its type, with walks for all abilities and an excellent selection of pubs that welcome walkers. *£6.95*

ORDERING INFORMATION

All of our books are available from your local bookshop. In case of difficulty, or to obtain our complete catalogue, please contact:

**SIGMA LEISURE,
1 South Oak Lane, Wilmslow, Cheshire SK9 6AR
Phone: 01625-531035   Fax: 01625-536800
E-mail: sigma.press@zetnet.co.uk**

ACCESS and VISA orders welcome. Please add £2 p&p to all orders.

**Free Catalogue on request. Or visit us on the World Wide Web -
http://www.sigmapress.co.uk**

(The web site generally contains more comprehensive information than our printed catalogue and is updated more frequently)